The Hennage Collection

American Antiques

The Hennage Collection

by

Elizabeth Stillinger

The Colonial Williamsburg Foundation

Williamsburg, Virginia

Distributed by Highland House Publishers, Alexandria, Virginia
Library of Congress Cataloging in Publication Data

Stillinger, Elizabeth.
    American antiques : the Hennage collection / by Elizabeth
Stillinger.
        p.   cm.
    Includes bibliographical references.
    ISBN 0-87935-080-6
    1. Antiques--United States--Catalogs. 2. Hennage, Joe--Art
collections--Catalogs. 3. Hennage, June--Art collections--Catalogs.
4. Antiques--Private collections--Virginia--Williamsburg--Catalogs.
I. Title.
NK806.S75   1990
745.1'0974'0747554252--DC20   90-38796
                                                      CIP

This book was designed by D. Richard Gallatin
Printed in the United States of America

Contents

Preface 1

Introduction 2

Collecting to Furnish a Home 4

The Entrance Stairhall 24

The Parlor 36

The Dining Room 58

The Library 84

The Charleston Bed and Sitting Rooms 96

The Upper Stairhall 109

The Private Rooms 116

A Home for the Collection 138

Afterword 149

Appendix 150

Bibliography 160

Preface

We in the museum field do not often have the pleasure of seeing the seeds we sow grow into full flower. Educators in an academic setting know who their students are, and they follow their subsequent progress in life. Pick up any alumni magazine and read the proud reports of successful alumni; in many ways the success of the graduates is the measure of the success of the school. Most museums, for better or worse, don't have the pleasure of knowing their visitors as individuals, and thus find it difficult to measure any long term contribution they might have made. The seeds are sown, and flowers bloom, but rarely can a direct cause and effect relationship be demonstrated. This book documents a wonderful exception to the general rule.

Joe and June Hennage came to love Colonial Williamsburg soon after they were married in 1947. It was, for them, a place of refuge and pleasure, an oasis of hospitality in which they could escape the workaday world. They came to love the style of Williamsburg as they spent more time here. It was, for them, a statement of urbanity, of beauty, and of grace. They came to love Colonial Williamsburg as a learning center as their commitment grew. Not only did they study the exhibition buildings, but they came with increasing frequency to the Antiques Forum, mining its rich veins of intellectual ore. They came to love Colonial Williamsburg, the home of great collections, as they themselves began to collect. Their decisions were often informed by the information that they had gleaned here. They have come to love Williamsburg as home, building their residence here and becoming neighbors as well as friends.

It is rare for a museum to have had such a clear, direct, and readily acknowledged influence on the development of a major collection. It is rarer still that the contribution of the museum should be so generously repaid. Joe and June Hennage have been deeply generous to a number of institutions, but to this one most of all. Their gifts have enriched the collections, as numbers of items have been given for display in the Historic Area and the Wallace Gallery of Decorative Arts. Their financial support of the Foundation has been equally generous. This generosity is clearly evident in the Wallace Gallery auditorium that bears their name, a wonderful space with state of the art equipment allowing the highest level of technical and aesthetic presentation. Their loyalty as boosters of Colonial Williamsburg has meant much to those of us who are working to see that the learning that has gone on here in the past will continue for the benefit of those who may come in the future. And finally, the bequest of their magnificent collection to Colonial Williamsburg is one of the most generous and important gifts in the long history of this organization. For that support, that vote of confidence, and for the opportunity it will provide to enlarge our role as educators of eighteenth-century culture, we are deeply grateful.

Charles R. Longsworth, President
Colonial Williamsburg Foundation

Introduction

This book is offered as an informal tour of June and Joe Hennage's outstanding collection of American antiques and complementary objects. The collection is presented first in room views that show it *in situ* at Hennage House on South England Street in Williamsburg, and then in separate illustrations that provide an opportunity for closer inspection of many individual pieces. The text combines general comments on the styles and forms shown with collecting stories and lore that relate to both the Hennages and earlier collectors.

So seldom have our collectors been profiled along with their collections that we Americans are accustomed to knowing virtually nothing about the motives and goals of the creators of our greatest antiques and art collections. It was in an effort to break that pattern and to capture the flavor of the collectors as well as of the collection that we chose the present format.

The book is divided into three parts. The first is a history of the Hennages' development as collectors within the framework of Colonial Williamsburg and its Antiques Forum, held there since 1949. The second is a full-color tour of Hennage House, the Georgian-style home that contains June and Joe's antiques. And the third is the story of planning and building Hennage House, which looks like a piece of the eighteenth century but functions like a piece of the late twentieth.

At the end of the volume is an appendix that includes specific information about materials, place of origin, maker or attribution, measurements, and provenance for each object shown, as well as other pertinent facts. The book is not meant to be a catalogue or a scholarly treatment of the Hennage collection—that will come later. It *is* meant to introduce an important assemblage of American antiques to curators, students, other collectors, and anyone else interested in American decorative arts in an accessible and interesting way.

Many people have contributed to this work. June and Joe Hennage were the most important, of course, and they were unfailingly helpful in sharing the documentation they have for each antique, in allowing me and Colonial Williamsburg's curators the freedom of the house to study objects, and in answering endless questions about both their antiques and their lives. In his capacity as this book's printer, Joe has gotten separations, layouts, and galleys back to us in record time. Bob Birney, Graham Hood, and John Sands worked with the Hennages and with me to formulate guidelines for the shape and content of this book, and Bob and John were consistently dependable sources of penetrating insight and advice throughout the period during which I wrote it. The copy was edited with diligence and vigilance by Donna Sheppard and Jan Gilliam.

Every member of Colonial Williamsburg's Collections Division provided assistance whenever I asked for it, and the book has benefited enormously from their contributions. John Austin, John Davis, Ron Hurst, and Margaret Pritchard selected groups of objects for illustration, recommended appropriate references, and answered many questions. Susan Shames introduced me to the Collections Division library and facilitated my borrowing whatever books I needed. Liza Gusler was invariably helpful in aiding me to find my way around the department and in suggesting resources, while Wallace Gusler very kindly considered notions about furniture collecting and collectors with me. Jon Prown joined Ron Hurst and me in peering at the undersides of tables, at drawer runners and dust boards—resulting in both a very good time and interesting new data. Trudy Moyles furnished background and reminiscences about the Antiques Forum that enriched my understanding of that phenomenon. Anne Verplanck very kindly filled me in on the current status of Ben Franklin's Franklin Court and sent me up-to-date research on miniature furniture. Emily Seats and Donna Tilghman responded to requests for reservations and other necessary arrangements promptly and efficiently, making my visits to Williamsburg unfailingly pleasant. Among my other friends in Williamsburg Elizabeth Blagojevich, Barbara Luck, Betty Leviner, and John Hyman saw that my off hours were filled with convivial company and good food and drink.

The photography in the book has come from several sources. Many of the individual pieces were shot by Joe Hennage himself, a reflection of his not inconsiderable talents in this area. Other pieces were shot by Hans Lorenz and Craig McDougal of the Colonial Williamsburg Collections Division; their skill in artifact photography is remarkable. Additional shots were the work of Dave Doody, Tom Austin, and Tom Green, of the Colonial Williamsburg Audiovisual Department. Finally, most of the room views at Hennage House are the work of Skip Baker of Williamsburg, who has succeeded admirably in capturing the ambience of the house.

Outside Colonial Williamsburg, Betsy and Wendell Garrett, Mary Humelsine, and Harold Sack very generously discussed the Hennage collection as well as the whole subject of collecting American antiques with me. Alice Winchester took time to read the essay on the Hennages as collectors and to make comments and corrections based on her long association with Colonial Williamsburg and the Antiques Forum. I am very grateful indeed for her help.

At home, my husband, Bill Guthman, and my two daughters, Alice and Amy Stillinger, provided comfort and good cheer, avoided interrupting (most of the time), read chapters as they rolled off the printer, and made dinners more often than not. They have, as always, my thanks and my love.

In the end, however, it is John Sands who deserves the credit for this book's existence. He set up the schedule and saw that we kept it; took charge of photography and kept impeccable track of transparencies and negatives; integrated points of view ranging from those of Colonial Williamsburg officialdom to those of the curators, the collectors, and the author; acted as editorial coordinator; and, usually, kept his cool. Toward the end, when we were discussing the almost-completed text and layout, Joe Hennage and I asked John if he liked what we'd wrought. He replied instantly and emphatically, "I like anything that's *finished*." Which, thanks to him, it now is.

Elizabeth Stillinger
Westport, Connecticut

Collecting to Furnish a Home

When June and Joe Hennage bought their first antique, "the antiques world" was emerging from a long period of dormancy. The collecting mania of the 1920s, when buyers battled on the auction floor and in the dealer's showroom, had receded as the Depression worsened. The *urge* to collect had not diminished, however, and while canny collectors such as Maxim Karolik and Bernice and Edgar Garbisch were picking up furniture and folk art at bargain prices, less well-off enthusiasts simply switched to less expensive antiques. Pressed glass and pewter, Alice Winchester has reminded us, came of age as respectable collectibles when Chippendale furniture was no longer an affordable option.

During World War II most people were too preoccupied to devote time to collecting antiques, and to many it seemed unpatriotic to pursue such a pleasurable pastime in the face of disastrous world events. But after the war the tide turned. Glad to be reunited and yearning to put the horrors of the late war behind them, families focused again on hearth and home.

Renewed interest in home implied also an absorption in furnishings and ambience. While "Danish Modern" appealed to many, "Early American" was a popular alternative. Americans' pride in their accomplishments here in the New World and their recently acknowledged global leadership strengthened their desire to learn about and live with things American. Opportunities to do just that increased, for this was the era in which a handful of huge private collections of American antiques first became available to the public. In Vermont it was Electra Havemeyer Webb's Shelburne Museum, consisting not only of the thousands of everyday and folk objects she had collected, but also of New England buildings that preserved the story of American architecture. In Massachusetts it was another outdoor museum, the Wells brothers' Old Sturbridge Village, made up of early nineteenth-century buildings from surrounding towns and countryside that contained the prodigious assortment of early tools, machinery, and implements they had assembled to tell the story of "Yankee ingenuity." In Delaware it was Henry Francis du Pont's Winterthur Museum, certainly the most prestigious and possibly the most influential collection-turned-museum of all. Du Pont's

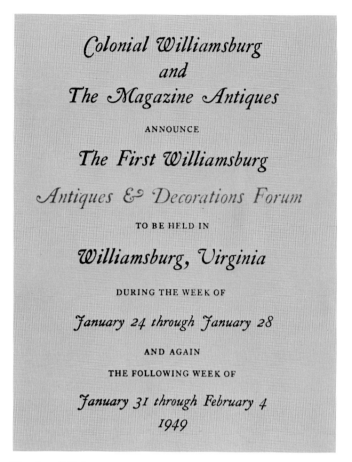

Colonial Williamsburg and The Magazine Antiques

ANNOUNCE

The First Williamsburg Antiques & Decorations Forum

TO BE HELD IN

Williamsburg, Virginia

DURING THE WEEK OF

January 24 through January 28

AND AGAIN

THE FOLLOWING WEEK OF

January 31 through February 4 1949

The first Williamsburg Antiques Forum started a long tradition.

interest was in form, color, texture, and all the other elements of design. He loved decorating, and he loved buying the objects and materials necessary to decorate. His museum was the house where he'd been born and raised, which he had transformed from an eclectic Victorian mansion into a colonial environment of over one hundred rooms furnished with an extraordinary collection of American antiques.

In 1949, correctly judging that Americans were ready to begin serious study of their material heritage, *The Magazine Antiques* and Colonial Williamsburg cosponsored the first Antiques Forum. It was there that many collectors important in their own regions but not always well known in the wider world began to meet and make friends with one another. An often cited example is the friendship of the genteel Miss Ima Hogg of Houston and the domineering Mrs. Katharine Prentis Murphy of New Hampshire, New York, and Connecticut. All this activity naturally inspired new collectors, and Joe and June Hennage were among them.

Joe Hennage was discharged from the United States Navy in 1945. He returned to Washington, D. C., and

Joe at work in his first printing business.

shortly thereafter bought out the printing company for which he had worked before the war. He started his own business with two presses and one employee besides himself. Having worked in the printing industry during his schooldays as well as immediately thereafter and throughout his period of service, he was a skilled craftsman. Probably even more important, he was filled with energy and ambition and was willing to pioneer new techniques, so his printing business soon began to prosper. In 1946, when he found himself in need of secretarial help, he hired June

Stedman, who had just finished school in Virginia and come to Washington to start a career. She ran the office, kept the books, and shared the boss's belief in his business.

Joe and June were married in 1947. Their first apartment gave no hint of their eventual environment, being in the blond wood "modern" style of the late forties and fifties. In their next home, a ranch-style house they built in the Washington suburbs, they supplemented the modern with a few colonial reproductions, for they had begun what turned out to be a lifelong addiction: trips to Colonial Williamsburg. They visited first in the late forties and were soon frequent guests at the Williamsburg Inn, which remained their favorite lodging place for many years.

Although June and Joe weren't present at the early sessions, Joe has often mentioned the great influence the Williamsburg Antiques Forum has had on them both. The Forum first convened in January 1949. Its speakers reflected the American antiques establishment of the day. The American Wing, the Smithsonian, Yale University, and the great English ceramics family of Wedgwood were represented, as was Colonial Williamsburg itself. Editors Alice Winchester and Charles Messer Stow gave lively evening lectures on collecting.

The sensation of that first Forum was Joseph Downs' talk. On the threshold of becoming the Winterthur Museum's first director but at the time still curator of the American Wing, Downs spoke on regional characteristics in early America, asserting that no colonial furniture worth collecting had been made south of Maryland. There was an immediate uproar, as Alice Winchester remembers it. One of the most voluble

The ranch house Joe and June built in 1949.

objectors, she says, was a young man from North Carolina who maintained that *of course* there was fine southern colonial furniture—he'd been collecting it since he was a lad.

As a result of all this furor, a movement was launched then and there that resulted, in 1952, in the first exhibition of southern decorative arts. It was held at the Virginia Museum of Fine Arts in Richmond and coordinated with an Antiques Forum devoted to lectures by the few knowledgeable students of the subject. Although that first exhibition and the complementary Forum program were crucial in surveying and introducing southern furniture to the American public, the subject is just now beginning to come of age—most notably as a result of the action taken by the young man from North Carolina. His name was Frank L. Horton, and he is the founder and guiding spirit of the outstanding Museum of Early Southern Decorative Arts in Winston-Salem, North Carolina. However, most of the collecting world, like Joe and June Hennage, didn't immediately seize on the idea of southern colonial antiques.

What attracted June, when she finally persuaded Joe to go into Arthur Vernay's elegant antiques emporium on New York's East 55th Street, was the lure not of the old South, nor even of colonial America, but of the elegant Georgian interiors of our English ancestors. Similar visions had influenced the first curators at Colonial Williamsburg in creating the rooms that June and Joe fell in love with during their initial visits to the restored capital. The story of their first antique purchase, the very handsome English tall clock now located on the main stairway, is given later. Suffice it to say here that Joe's first shocked reaction to the price of a fine antique has been tempered substantially by his subsequent dealings with members of the antiques-dealers fraternity.

The Hennages' first visit to Mr. Vernay occurred in 1963, and Joe's daily association with the elaborately marquetried clock soon converted him to the pleasures of living with antiques. He and June acquired a number of other pieces, all English, and then one day in 1965 June walked into an antiques shop at 5 East 57th Street and discovered American antiques.

Though the firm still bore (and bears) his name, Israel Sack, its founder and probably the most renowned of all early dealers in American decorative arts, had by this time passed the business along to his three sons. That day June met Harold, the eldest brother and the one who heads the company. He showed her around the shop and talked to her about the

Pamela Copeland and Frank Horton visited the 1952 exhibition of southern furniture, sponsored by the Virginia Museum and Colonial Williamsburg.

special qualities of American antiques. June left knowing that Joe would like and respect Harold Sack because she had a feeling he understood business and businessmen. If Joe could deal with men like Harold, she thought, he would soon become interested in collecting antiques.

In 1965 the antiques world was still connected in many ways to the "good old days" of the early years of this century, when many of the most famous American collections were formed. Although the early greats like Israel Sack of Boston and New York; Ginsburg & Levy, originally of New York's Lower East Side and later of Madison Avenue; Charles Woolsey Lyon and his son (of the same name), of New York and, after the financial reverses of the Great Depression caught up with them, of Millbrook, New York; Flayderman and Kauffman of Boston, vendors of American antiques of the highest caliber until the Depression wiped them out; Arthur Sussell, for many years the leading antiques dealer in Philadelphia; and the crafty "Old Prior" of Hartford had passed on, there were still many wonderful early dealers on the scene.

Joe Kindig, Jr., equal in fame, almost, to Israel Sack, kept shop in York, Pennsylvania; Rocky Gardiner pursued his eccentric and always fascinating researches into American antiques of every description in Stamford, Connecticut; Devere Card, to the end an astute and precise judge of quality, ran his business amid what appeared to be, until one was invited to view the neatly arranged treasures upstairs, a sea of old newspapers in upstate New York; John Walton, part American Indian, he said, and all sure instinct for the best in American furniture, did business in Connecticut and New York; Nathan Liverant held forth in Colchester, Connecticut; Fred Johnston, purveyor of wonderful Hudson River Valley furnishings, was established in Kingston, New York; and many others just as astute but often less well known traded in superior American antiques.

The ladies, too, had come into their own. Among them, Elinor Gordon offered China trade porcelain of the highest quality in Villanova, Pennsylvania; Lillian Ullman proffered enchanting folk art in a big house overlooking the Hudson in Tarrytown, New York; Florene Maine sold classic examples of American furniture in her colonial house on the old "antiques highway," Route 7, in Ridgefield, Connecticut; Mary Allis not only sold but helped create the mythology of American folk art, first in New York and later in Southport, Connecticut; Lillian Blankley Cogan supplied seventeenth- and eighteenth-century chairs and chests, delft and slipware to many of the early collectors from *her* big old house in Farmington, Connecticut; Helena Penrose tempted buyers into her New York and Southbury, Connecticut, shops, which she advertised as the "headquarters for Americana"; and Marguerite Riordan presented New England furniture and folk art in Stonington, Connecticut.

Among the dealers, as among all other groups, some were more beloved than others, some considered tricky, some scholarly, some intuitive, some merely shrewd, but all contributed to the growth—indeed, to the actual shape and fiber—of the American antiques world. Some of them began to lecture, first at the Antiques Forum and later at other similar gatherings, for it was they who had sought out and cultivated sources, learned to distinguish the good from the better and the best, and gathered the objects that formed many of the great early collections. Many of them, too, had educated their clients and taught them connoisseurship. Here, at the Forum, was a podium for them, where they could share their knowledge and pass it along to future generations.

Since this was the first event based on lectures by experts in different categories of antiques, it also offered the first opportunity for collectors to listen to, meet, and exchange ideas with curators of the museums that shaped their knowledge and taste. Jim Cogar, Williamsburg's first curator, spoke at the first Forum, as did Minor Wine Thomas, also of Colonial Williamsburg, Joe Downs of the American Wing, Malcolm Watkins of the Smithsonian, John Marshall Phillips of the Yale University Art Gallery, and Charles Montgomery, soon to be of the Winterthur Museum.

Collectors, too, were invited to speak at the Forum.

Other participants were fascinated by their collecting tales and informed by their knowledge of the material they gathered. Nina Fletcher Little, then and now one of New England's premier collectors, spoke at the first Forum and at every subsequent Forum for at least ten years. Ralph Carpenter of Scarsdale, New York, collector of Rhode Island furniture, and Maxim Karolik of Boston and Newport, collector of fine high-style furniture and American paintings, were other speakers in the early years. More recently, Joe Hennage has spoken about his collection both at Williamsburg and at other collectors' gatherings, but it wasn't until the early sixties that he and June began to attend the entire week of Antiques Forum sessions.

Although Joe has always appreciated the American past, he and June began collecting not antiques, but memorabilia relating to Benjamin Franklin, Joe's hero since boyhood, and books on printing, the trade they shared. When they presented this collection to the Earl Gregg Swem Library at the College of William and Mary in 1981, it contained more than 230 volumes covering 500 years of printing history and art. Joe admired Franklin's inventiveness—a characteristic that implies a lively mind and an unwillingness to settle for inadequate solutions—and he shares that trait. In fact, this is an unusual case in which an antiquarian hero leads straight to a modern working environment. Since he began in business, Joe has looked for the most up-to-date and efficient methods of running his company, which rapidly expanded from printing to include design, advertising, and mail-order departments. Joe's brand of inventiveness combines the will to build a better mousetrap with the conviction that you must also *tell people that you have done so*. Harold Sack, who probably knows him as well as anyone, says that Joe's special genius is for promotion.

Harold remembers vividly one instance of Joe's promotional talents. A lawyer, representing the author's family, had left with the Sacks the text and photographic negatives for the well-known *Blue Book, Philadelphia Furniture*, written by William M. Hornor, Jr., and published in a small edition in 1935. Though it is by now over fifty years old, the *Blue Book* remains an authoritative and widely used source. The material sat unnoticed until Joe spotted it and asked Harold Sack about it. When Harold told him, Joe immediately decided to arrange for publication rights. That accomplished, he formed Highland House Publishers and reprinted the *Blue Book*, which until then had been available only to those with $200 to spend in the rare book market. With the successful republication of Hornor's book behind him, Joe moved on to *American Antiques from the Israel Sack Collection,* a series currently numbering nine volumes, in which he consolidates Sack's heavily illustrated sales brochures "every two years or 250 pages." In addition, each volume contains reprinted articles or retrospective essays on collecting or market trends by one of the Sack brothers. They have included major reviews of the collections at the White House and the Diplomatic Reception Rooms of the State Department. These books, too, have sold successfully. One auction house expert recently said that she would never think of cataloging furniture for a sale without first searching the *American Antiques* series for similar pieces.

It is his promotional ability that has enabled Joe—always with June's support and encouragement—to build the business from a two-person effort to the present sixty-employee operation, now called Hennage Creative Printers. Fifteen years after founding the company, Joe wrote of his "modern, self-contained plant with its own art studio, camera and plate labs, and the latest and best printing, binding and electronic mailing machinery." The plant was organized to meet the needs of the customers Joe sought—those who, like himself, were unusually demanding in the areas of service and quality. A printing industry publication reported at the time that "the Hennage company can almost literally pick a job out of the customer's mind and process it completely for delivery to him or to the Post Office without ever having it leave the plant."

The modern interior of Joe's second plant stands in stark contrast to his earlier premises.

A bronze bust of Joe by sculptor Robert Berks illustrated the cover story.

A certificate of appreciation presented to Joe by the British Federation of Master Printers; it is engrossed by hand on vellum.

This situation was owing not just to modern facilities and state-of-the-art equipment, but also to Joe's conviction that money's not the problem, *ideas* are the problem. He believes that if you offer your customers new and interesting ideas, the business will follow. He made this point some years ago in a speech to the British Federation of Master Printers, maintaining that the key ingredient in his own success was creativity—serving his customers by developing ideas to meet their goals and solve their problems. To demonstrate, Joe pulled a slip of paper from his pocket. He showed the audience that the word "Ideas" was printed on the paper, which he then dropped into a bowl of water. The slip dissolved, leaving the word "Ideas" floating on the surface to prove that ideas are more durable than paper.

In 1968 he was elected president of the Master Printers of America. In 1970 he became chairman of the board of the Printing Industries of America, a 14,000-company industry organization. Each of these organizations subsequently recognized his contributions to the field by naming him "Man of the Year." In these situations as in his business, community service, and avocations, Joe worked diligently at the day-to-day tasks while coming up with new ideas for developing and strengthening programs and creating goodwill. Other organizations Joe has served as an officer include the Boys Clubs of America and the Optimists Clubs. When asked his reason for giving so much time to service organizations, Joe says simply, "When you take, you ought to give back."

One event Joe organized as a tribute to the printing profession in general and to Ben Franklin in particular was a luncheon held during Printing Week, 1968, for Washington civic and business leaders. Guests enjoyed an eighteenth-century menu featuring "quail in the basket," a chance to pay their respects to the extremely lifelike Dr. Franklin borrowed for the occasion from Washington's Wax Museum, and a short talk on Franklin as a printer by Dr. Leonard W. Larabee, Franklin scholar from Yale.

Joe is honored as 1968 Man of the Year by the Master Printers of America; he appears with Norman Vincent Peale.

June and Joe at an Optimists Club dinner, Hotel Roanoke.

Ben Franklin is served at the Hennage's party, City Tavern, Georgetown.

Dr. Franklin, on loan from the Washington Wax Museum, appears in his re-created printing shop.

The north end of the living room in the house in Kenwood.

Joe highlighted Franklin in another promotion the next year: a release from Hennage Creative Printers announced that Ben Franklin, master printer, had reopened his shop for business in the Hennage building at 9th and H Streets, N.W. Situated in the lobby, the re-created colonial printshop contained a Washington handpress, type case, and other equipment as well as a representation of Franklin himself.

June, an important partner in the Hennage company from the beginning, has also combined outside interests with her business and personal responsibilities. Gardening is one of her great pleasures, and Colonial Williamsburg has been a formative influence here, too. One interviewer speaks of the "well-planned Williamsburg garden with statuary and great attention to detail" when describing the Hennages' second house, which they built in Kenwood, a private community in Chevy Chase, Maryland.

In the late fifties, when the Hennages planned and built this second house, the period room, an approach

to furnishing popularized first by the American Wing and then by Colonial Williamsburg and Winterthur, was in its heyday. The period room technique was an extension of the environmentally accurate cases in natural history museums in which birds and other forms of wildlife were shown surrounded by the flora and fauna characteristic of their natural habitats. In decorative arts displays this meant providing an architectural setting of the same date as the furniture and other objects used in the room, so that the viewer could see that things made of different materials but during the same stylistic period exhibited the same lines and decorative motifs.

The importance of the period room was that it provided a context for collections of antiques. Its immense popularity stemmed from the fact that it worked in private homes just as well as it did in institutions like Colonial Williamsburg. Several generations of collectors formed their mental pictures of proper eighteenth-century American interiors by as-

The house in Kenwood, Chevy Chase, Maryland.

The garden at the Kenwood house.

similating the lessons of such period rooms. Colors, textures, and patterns for walls and fabrics, styles of carpets, arrangements of furnishings, and a pervading sense of richness—all were there to be absorbed. What curator John Davis describes as the clublike atmosphere of the first several Forums fostered friendships between collectors and curators that encouraged an easy exchange of ideas and information. While the curators' major responsibility, of course, was the care and exhibition of the Williamsburg collections, their friendships with collectors made it very natural for them to consult with collector friends about new acquisitions and decorative and furnishing schemes.

Postwar Americans' desire to concentrate on home and family meant that Williamsburg was in a unique position. It was both the perfect place for a family vacation and—once the family had arrived—the perfect place to pick up new ideas about houses and furnishings within an entirely American context. Here was a whole town full of houses containing furniture, silver, ceramics, glass, pewter, and other objects of the same period as the architecture. Private collectors were delighted with these visual blueprints for charming homes whose outsides matched their insides and whose landscaping was in keeping with both. Jim Cogar and his successor, John Graham, chief curator during the two decades after the war, were the principal architects of this "Williamsburg look."

In providing a complete home environment, Williamsburg had a real advantage over the American Wing, where only interiors were on view. Perhaps best of all, many of the elements that made the restored houses so appealing were for sale in reproduction form at the Williamsburg Craft House, the retail outlet next to the Historic Area. Begun in the 1930s, the Colonial Williamsburg reproductions program, in which the curators worked with carefully selected producers of paint, wallpaper, fabrics, furniture, ceramics, pewter, and other types of materials to create high quality reproductions, was the first—and undoubtedly the most successful—of all the museum reproductions programs.

The Hennages' house in Kenwood, a lovely warm-red brick dwelling in the Georgian manner, exemplified the Williamsburg style: its exterior and interior details were coordinated, and the surrounding lawns and gardens complemented the architecture. When the Hennages built the house in 1958 they had not yet begun collecting antiques, but they strengthened their sense of identity with Williamsburg by furnishing it with reproductions from the Craft House and by hanging a series of watercolor views of Williamsburg, which they commissioned over a period of twenty years, in their family room.

June's interest in gardening led her to become actively involved in the Kenwood Garden Club: over the years she has organized numerous events and served as president, while winning blue ribbons along the way. The Washington Club, a women's group in the District of Columbia, is another of her concerns. Recently, when the club building needed a new roof, June asked Joe to speak at a fund-raising dinner. He agreed, and his lecture about building and furnishing Hennage House in Williamsburg drew a crowd whose contributions got the fund-raising drive off to a splendid start. June has always been willing to contribute time and effort to Joe's causes, too, and to head up women's events at printing industry meetings. For one Washington-based conference, she arranged a trip to Mount Vernon, a tour of the house and grounds, and a return journey complete with music and champagne. She is a masterly party giver, having held many

The living room in the house in Kenwood.

June with one of her garden club displays, a blue ribbon effort.

June entertains printing executives at Mount Vernon.

amples with flowers, with strawberries in season, and with myriad other things that need an attractive container. For a spring luncheon one year, June heaped Easter candies into tiny baskets and set one at each place as a favor. "I think baskets go with everything from formal to rustic," she says, "and I love to send them to friends filled with flowers. Joe calls it 'basket mania.'" When they were building their new house in Williamsburg, Joe designed and installed plexiglass shelves just below the cornice in the kitchen so that June could display her collection to best advantage.

For many years June has also been buying what she and Joe call "penny toys," and by now they have accumulated a collection that can stand on its own. Each Christmas the toys come out of storage to decorate the tree and the room in which it stands. Miniature animals, vehicles, and figures perch on branches, scurry about under the tree, and parade along the upper sill of the French doors. One year Joe photographed the tree in company with their marquetried tall clock and one of June's miniature chairs and used the picture for their Christmas card. It was such a hit that people who hadn't received a card called to ask if they could have one!

June's love of all kinds of small objects explains her attraction to toys—and also to miniature furniture. Her collection of diminutive tables, chests, chairs, and beds is remarkable for its quality and range of forms. "The workmanship is extraordinary," she says, adding that she is captivated by miniatures because they required at least as much skill and effort to make as pieces of ordinary size. Perhaps miniatures were even more difficult to create, she feels, because it was so important to get their scale right.

By the late sixties, Joe and June had been collecting American antiques for several years and had occasion-

admirably organized and beautifully decorated lunches, teas, and dinners over the years. She and Joe both love lavish black-tie parties at which, in the last ten or so years, they've been able to use their collections of furniture and silver to maximum potential.

A party is a perfect opportunity for creative thinking, and the Hennages are fully alive to the imaginative possibilities. At one dinner they passed out the names of famous couples. Instead of finding your seat by means of an ordinary place card, you were asked to search out your historical partner. If you were Lancelot, for example, you'd go looking for Guinevere. When you found her and took your seat at her side, you might also find Martha and George Washington, Josephine and Napoleon, Helen of Troy and Paris, and Tarzan and Jane sharing your table. Later on, fortified by June's elegant food and rare vintages from Joe's wine cellar, you were asked to comment on the evening from the point of view of your historical *persona.*

June is also creative in her use of the smaller collections she has formed. She fills baskets from her large assemblage of old, new, and in-between ex-

Dinner for the Humelsines in Chevy Chase.

The Hennages love to entertain.

ally attended the Antiques Forum. The theme in 1964, the first year they had registered for a complete session, was "The Four Corners of the Earth and American Antiques," and among the speakers were specialists on oriental ceramics, which has become one of June's great interests. As early as the 1950s she and Joe were collecting antique Chinese bronzes, porcelain, snuff bottles, and netsuke, much of which they have since given to the Virginia Museum of Fine Arts in Richmond. The next Forum for which she and Joe registered was that held in 1969, when the theme was specifically "The Oriental Impulse in Early America." Speakers focused on Chinese porcelains, on oriental lacquer wares and rugs, and on "Toys as History," other areas in which June and Joe have become involved as collectors.

The Williamsburg Antiques Forum has probably had more influence on America's collecting tastes and ideas about the past than any comparable institution except the American Wing, which opened its doors to widespread acclaim in 1924. Winterthur, too, has shaped our concepts about early American life, but in the beginning it was not so widely publicized as the other two and was therefore not so influential (another demonstration of the validity of Joe's belief that success results as much from publicity as from the product itself). The only other organization that consistently focused on themes in American collecting was *The Magazine Antiques,* published from 1922 onward. It was Homer Eaton Keyes, *Antiques'* first editor and a true connoisseur and collector himself, who first looked at what his countrymen were collecting and sought out experts to write about it. Mr. Keyes also instituted monthly write-ups of coming events, reports and reviews of current shows, auctions, and exhibitions, and timely reminders of and comments on

all the other occurrences in the world of antiques. As an ongoing encyclopedia and calendar of events, *The Magazine Antiques* became necessary to anyone with an interest in American decorative arts.

Twenty-seven years after the magazine's founding, Mr. Keyes's assistant, Alice Winchester, who had become editor upon his death in 1938, collaborated with Colonial Williamsburg's staff to provide another source of up-to-date information on American and English decorative arts. Like *Antiques,* the Forum offered a chance to find out first-hand what collectors and scholars were thinking and acquiring—and why. And *un*like *Antiques,* it offered an unprecedented opportunity to get to know others with similar interests. For the first time ever it offered collectors, curators, dealers, and scholars from North America and Europe the opportunity not only to share their ideas and knowledge, but to get to know one another personally for a week or two each year.

Actually, there *is* one organization older than the Forum that brings members of the American decorative and fine arts communities together. The Walpole Society, an elite group of gentlemen collectors and curators, was founded in 1909 and held its first meeting in Hartford, Connecticut, in 1910. The Society had no fixed meeting place, so each spring and fall one or more members would arrange a Walpole weekend near his home, ensuring new and different sights at each gathering. The Society's emphasis is on looking rather than lecturing—though good *talk* has always been important—and in this respect it is obviously very different from the Antiques Forum.

In spirit, however, early Forum meetings had much in common with early Walpole Society meetings. The enthusiasm Judge John Woolsey conveyed in his report of a long-ago meeting sounds very like an old-

June's collection of baskets.

Alice Winchester of *Antiques* **chats with Joe Kindig, Jr., 1952 Antiques Forum.**

timer's description of Forum life in the fifties: "What a great reunion! And such a good time! and what a fine collection of clocks and old furniture. . . ." Visiting private collections has always been a major feature of Walpole Society meetings, and the group maintained that tradition during a recent trip to Virginia by arranging a visit with the Hennages. Joe reports, with enthusiasm matching Judge Woolsey's, that he's rarely had such fun as he had discussing woods, finishes, construction techniques, and regional characteristics with various Walpoleans.

The major differences between the Society and the Forum, however, are in the areas of size and exclusiveness. The Forum is open to all, while one of the Society's main characteristics is its exclusivity. That used to matter much more than it does now, when there are so many collector- and museum-sponsored events that no one need feel excluded from any one group. The Forum's great advantage is that *any* interested collector or would-be collector can meet others who share his particular interests, make new friends among speakers, Williamsburg staff, and other Forum participants, and, by taking copious notes, come away with a good basic survey of the theme subject.

In the beginning the Forum audience was a couple of hundred—small and informal enough for everyone to get acquainted—and it is those early years that Forum regulars remember with nostalgia. "We had such fun," says one, "we had wonderful parties—even pillow fights in the halls of the Inn! And when the Forum was over, we all visited one another at home." She recalls one session in the early fifties when Joe Kindig, Jr., was speaking. A group that included Hensleigh Wedgwood, head of the American office of his family's renowned pottery, was assembled for cocktails in Kindig's room at the Inn. After a period

Hensleigh Wedgwood examines a ceramic piece, held by an unidentified guest, while Nina Fletcher Little looks on, 1949 Antiques Forum.

of refreshment, Wedgwood removed his shoes and socks, placed a pen between his toes, and sketched his host's portrait on a nearby patch of wallpaper. "It looked just like him too," recalls Wedgwood's fellow reveler.

Hensleigh Wedgwood had spoken at the very first Forum and had become a member of a group of "Forum regulars" that returned year after year. Another occasional speaker and member of the group was Maxim Karolik, one of the most colorful figures in the history of American antiques collecting. Karolik was tall, with impressive features and a commanding presence. He was born in Russia in 1893 and studied drama and voice there until 1918, when he fled the Bolshevik regime. When he arrived in America in 1922, he had no assets except his belief in himself and his splendid tenor voice.

Although the operatic career he hoped for never materialized, Karolik did make his fortune with his voice. He partially supported himself by singing operatic arias after dinner at private parties, and in this capacity he was present at an upper-crust dinner in Washington, D. C., attended by Martha Codman, a very proper Boston spinster. Whether she was captivated by his looks, his voice, or his self-assured manner is not known, but captivated Miss Codman was. In short order she, a Brahmin of enviable wealth and social position, and Maxim Karolik, a Russian immigrant half her age, eloped. They wisely set off immediately for an extended honeymoon in Europe, preventing the bride's incredulous relatives from interfering.

Upon their return Karolik, being a man of both words and deeds, soon took positive action to express his admiration of America's independent spirit and democratic institutions. His wife had inherited some of the loveliest furniture made in and around Boston in the colonial and early Federal periods. Using that as a core, Karolik began assembling a collection of the finest examples he could find of eighteenth- and early nineteenth-century high-style American furniture with the express purpose of giving it to the Museum of Fine Arts, Boston. He was eminently successful, and as the years went on he became a fixture in Boston society, as much a part of the setting as the matrons who flocked to his lectures on the Karolik collections. "All my bobby soxers are over fifty," he used to say.

When the furniture collection was complete, Karolik formed two more major groups for the Museum: one of nineteenth-century paintings and another of nineteenth-century prints, drawings, and watercolors. He was, wrote Brian O'Doherty, "an American insti-

Katharine Prentis Murphy talks with Mrs. Henderson, a hostess at the Wythe House, 1949 Antiques Forum.

tution. He is one of the few American institutions born in Russia, who can tell a joke and the difference between a Boston and a Philadelphia tall-boy." These were qualities—along with his keen artistic eye—that put Karolik at the center of the social scene at all the Forums he attended.

Also regulars, though they were all well up in years when the Antiques Forum began, were Katharine Prentis Murphy, Ima Hogg, and Electra Havemeyer Webb, who became fast friends as a result of attending together. Mrs. Murphy, like Karolik a commanding personality, was as spirited a party giver as she was a collector, and once she got to know interested people outside her New York circle she was instrumental in creating a cohesive group of collectors of American antiques. She entertained at both her New York apartment and her old house in Connecticut—always with great flair. Flair characterized Mrs. Murphy's decorative schemes, too—the theme was European in her New York rooms, Early American in her Connecticut farmhouse. There, banister-back chairs, gateleg tables, blue and white delft chargers, pewter tankards, and oriental rugs were combined to form colorful, atmospheric interiors that inspired many a younger collector. Though her antiques were not always innocent of the restorer's hand, they invariably *looked* wonderful. She was a generous donor to museums and historical societies in New England and New York, and she was equally generous to her friends, though she had an imperious, domineering side as well.

Ima Hogg of Houston, Texas, became particularly good friends with Katharine Murphy, and they used to talk by phone every Sunday night. Miss Ima's family had struck oil early in the century, and as a result she was able to buy antiques at the most exalted price levels. She and her brother Will had begun to collect in the twenties, but upon his death in the early thirties she lost interest in the pursuit. In the 1950s, she decided to turn her home, Bayou Bend, into a museum and began collecting with renewed vigor. With the help of John Graham, then chief curator at Colonial Williamsburg, and as a tribute to her friend Katharine, Miss Ima created (among many other rooms) the New Hampshire parlor at Bayou Bend. Anyone familiar with Katharine Murphy's old farmhouse immediately recognized her decorative trademarks in the New Hampshire parlor's energetically scrolled William and Mary furniture and bold black and white floor (she took the idea from the floor treatment in *Alice Mason*, a seventeenth-century child's portrait now in the Adams house in Quincy, Massachusetts).

Electra Webb, friend of both Miss Ima and Katharine Murphy, was another of the leading collectors of the day. She had been brought up with European old masters and impressionists and had appalled her mother by choosing to collect American folk art rather than the more "important" art she had known as a child. But she had a remarkably forward-looking sense of what represented the American character, and she collected it unerringly throughout her lifetime. In 1947 she brought her collection together at the Shelburne Museum in northern Vermont, where it was displayed in New England houses that are also part of the story of early America.

Henry Francis du Pont was the most outstanding collector in America at the time of the early Forums, and although he was friends with many who became regulars, he was not one himself. When asked why he had not joined in, a loyal Forum goer replied, "Well, you know, he was always kind of odd." Which is to say, perhaps, that he never was much of a joiner or wholehearted supporter of projects other than his own.

Among others who came were Edgar and Bernice Chrysler Garbisch, Ralph and Cynthia Carpenter, Henry and Helen Flynt, Pamela Copeland, and Harry du Pont's sister, Louise Crowninshield—all from the East, all collectors, and most involved with museums.

Alice Winchester and Mrs. George M. Morris examine a cup at the Governor's Palace, 1949 Antiques Forum.

Among those professionally involved in American decorative arts were Alice Winchester and Helen Comstock from *Antiques;* Marshall and Petey Davidson, he head of the Metropolitan Museum publications department and she of *Antiques;* John Marshall Phillips, curator of the Garvan Collection at Yale and creator of the famous decorative arts course nicknamed "pots and pans"; Esther and Donald Shelley, director of the Henry Ford Museum; Charles and Florence Montgomery of Winterthur, he a visionary museum man and she a leading historical textiles scholar; and Dean and M'Lou Fales, he director of the Essex Institute and she a Winterthur-trained silver expert.

Lloyd Hyde was another regular—a charming man who was good friends with many leading collectors of the day and who, Alice Winchester says, "inspired a special group of 15-20 collectors to gather at one anothers' homes (restorations) for pleasant weekend parties. The collectors loved to entertain each other—and to vie with one another." Lloyd Hyde sold interesting and exotic antiques from his beautifully decorated New York apartment; he had been one of the first to go to the Orient looking for China trade porcelain, and he spoke on that subject at the Forum.

Nina and Bert Little of Brookline, Massachusetts, came, too, though they don't fit neatly into one cate-

gory: besides being ardent collectors of New England antiques of all kinds, each was seriously involved professionally. Nina Little's interest in the history of her antiques led her into significant research on New England art and culture, resulting in many articles and books, while Bert was for many years director of the Society for the Preservation of New England Antiquities. From Colonial Williamsburg itself there were the Humelsines, the Chorleys, the Alexanders, the Gonzales, and John Graham.

Cincinnati, Chicago, and Denver were represented, too, and there were many Southerners, including Frank Horton of North Carolina, the Henry Greens of Georgia, and groups from Atlanta, North Carolina, Mississippi, and Texas, as well as from other parts of the Midwest and South. From the Washington area in the early years came the Congers, the Joynts, the Mourots, Mrs. George Maurice Morris, and the Blagojeviches, as well as the Hennages from the mid-sixties on. They were regulars—sometimes speakers—at the Forum, and all were influential members of the American antiques world of the fifties and sixties. Their taste was influenced by what they saw and heard in Williamsburg, and they, in turn, influenced many other collectors.

Besides illustrating architectural and decorative styles, the Williamsburg Historic Area also provided Forum speakers with a context for their remarks. The Governor's Palace, residences such as the George Wythe and Peyton Randolph houses, and the various craft shops and taverns, all furnished according to the decorative arts and period room wisdom of the day, served as supplementary texts to speakers' comments. Whether they referred to this background specifically or simply presupposed their audience's awareness of it, speaker and context worked together. Unless, of course, the speaker chose to disagree with the context, in which case it still served a purpose.

Now, in many cases, scholarship has moved on and the backgrounds have changed, but collectors accustomed to the earlier environments have not always changed accordingly. This has created dissension in some quarters, causing both the institutions and the protesting collectors to examine their positions—not necessarily an unhealthy situation. Some collectors who had attended the Forum since the beginning were so distressed at the changes new research and study in the late seventies made necessary in the room arrangements of the Governor's Palace that they simply stopped attending the Forum. They had identified so deeply with the cozier, more conventionally charming

A group from the first Antiques Forum, 1949, visits the Governor's Palace.

Miodrag and Elizabeth Blagojevich talk with Ernest Donnelly and May Joynt, 1951 Antiques Forum.

approach of earlier years—an approach they had in many cases adopted for their own homes and for museums and historic houses with which they were involved—that they felt personally affronted by the changes. June Hennage, while by no means upset enough to miss the Forum, has said that she too prefers the luxurious look of earlier days to the more severe look of the present. And it is the traditional path that she and Joe have taken in furnishing Hennage House, their new home in Williamsburg.

With the arrival of the 1970s and their regular attendance at the Antiques Forum, June and Joe began to collect American antiques at a faster pace. A few years earlier Joe had been asked to serve on the Fine Arts Committee of the State Department, a group formed to aid White House and State Department curator Clement Conger in raising funds for the architectural renovation and furnishing of the diplomatic reception rooms. As Joe's first service to the committee, he volunteered to design and print, at his own expense, a full-color booklet showing before and after pictures of

the reception rooms as a way of publicizing the State Department project. The brochure, which included particulars for those interested in making contributions, was most successful in recruiting new donors, although Stanley Stone of Milwaukee, a long-time Forum regular and collector, spoke out against the undertaking. Stone chose to present his views at a dinner at Carter's Grove, a plantation that is now part of Colonial Williamsburg. "I don't like the idea of gathering all those priceless things together where they might be damaged by the public," he said. Some collectors and dealers agreed with him, but most, including the Hennages, felt it was more important for America's foreign guests to be entertained in settings filled with the best of our material heritage than to be too protective. As a result of his successful contribution, Joe received the first certificate the Secretary of State presented "In recognition of a generous contribution to the preservation and display of our American Heritage of Design and Decorative Arts. . . ."

In addition, June and Joe have given the State De-

June and Clem Conger with the tall clock the Hennages donated to the State Department, 1969; the eagle inlay is particularly noteworthy.

June and Joe with the bombé chest they gave to the State Department; compare with the interior paneling of the previous view to understand why the project was so necessary.

June, chairman of the first Washington Antiques Show loan exhibition, is seated with Mrs. Morris and Harold Sack.

Joe introduces the Americana project for the National Archives, 1972.

partment many fine pieces of American furniture. Among them are a Boston bombé and a Virginia serpentine chest of drawers, a chest-on-chest made for New York's Van Rensselaer family, a Virginia tea table, two New York Chippendale chairs, a Massachusetts Queen Anne easy chair, a Federal tall clock attributed to Matthew Egerton of New Jersey, and a miniature of Ben Franklin. The areas of the State Department these objects furnish have been transformed from grim, boxlike spaces into elegantly paneled and pilastered rooms painted in warm, attractive colors. Furnishings, both donated and on loan, are in the tradition of Williamsburg and Winterthur period rooms of the fifties, sixties, and seventies.

All furnishings are in the Queen Anne, Chippendale, and Federal styles, and each object is the most fashionable of its era, as seems fitting for rooms in which affairs of state are managed. Imported crystal chandeliers, China trade ceramics, oriental rugs, and silk fabrics in period patterns complement the Ameri-

can furniture, paintings, prints, and silver.

Joe's involvement in this enterprise led to his being asked to head two other Americana drives—one for the National Archives and the other for the Supreme Court. Heading the National Archives Americana committee was a job that suited Joe perfectly. Not only is he an excellent fund-raiser, but as a printer he is also fascinated by the Archives' contents—priceless American documents such as the Declaration of Independence, the United States Constitution, the Bill of Rights, and many other records, letters, and texts of great importance, some in manuscript and some in printed form.

The purpose of Joe's committee, formed in 1972, was to acquire from descendants of the Signers of the Declaration of Independence, the Constitution, and other sources furnishings, works of art, memorabilia, and archival material known to have belonged to people associated with those documents. A related goal was to create room settings that re-created the periods when these important documents were written. At a dinner the Hennages gave to celebrate the launching of the Americana project, Joe and his committee (composed of other leading collectors and museum people) unveiled a room in the Federal style. Containing objects made between 1783, the end of the American Revolution, and 1825, the year John Quincy Adams became president and General Lafayette, French hero of the American Revolution, concluded a triumphal tour of America, the room represented an era in which an unprecedented number of historic American documents were conceived and executed.

The Supreme Court assignment was similar to the other two: Chief Justice Warren Burger had asked Joe to put together a series of rooms for the justices to use on special occasions. Much like State Department officials, Supreme Court justices are constantly receiving visits from representatives of judicial courts around the world. Joe's job was to secure private funds and donations that he could use to create handsome, comfortable rooms furnished with fine American antiques and paintings.

During the Bicentennial year, June and Joe made an extraordinary number of important gifts to American institutions. One of the most significant was a four-page letter of 1796 from George Washington to Gustavus Scott of Philadelphia, which the Hennages presented to Mount Vernon. The letter expresses Washington's views on developments in Washington, D.C., soon to be the nation's capital city. Another letter, which the Hennages gave to Monticello, Thomas

Jefferson's beloved home, is from Jefferson to Virginia's Governor John Page. In it, Jefferson expresses concern about the country's first counterfeiting ring and the effect it will have on the economy. Other gifts included a letter from President John Adams, to the Massachusetts Historical Society; a marble statue of Franklin after Caffiéri, to the White House; a cast of Franklin after Houdon, to the National Portrait Gallery; and a Chippendale looking glass made circa 1775 for William Van Rensselaer of Albany, New York, to Colonial Williamsburg.

The Hennages' active participation in these patriotic projects naturally increased their knowledge of American antiques and brought them into contact with many others who shared their interests. Both June and Joe give Harold Sack great credit for his help in forming their furniture collection, but they began attending antiques shows and getting to know other dealers as well. Not surprisingly, they became active in two local shows; Joe serves as a national trustee of the Baltimore Museum, which sponsors a yearly show,

and one year, June was chairperson of the first loan exhibition held in connection with the Washington antiques show.

Their own collection grew briskly, expanding to include American and English silver, oriental rugs, China trade porcelain, and accessories such as chandeliers, andirons, and candlesticks. They occasionally bought still-life and genre paintings that appealed to them, and recently they have been buying fine early maps of Virginia and other colonies. Pieces of less than top quality were weeded out as it became possible to buy finer ones. "When we started buying antiques," June has said, "we had no idea that collecting would turn out to be such a major part of our lives."

June *has* had a lifelong interest in houses and furniture, though. "I never get tired of walking in the city and looking at buildings," she says. "I can walk along the same streets every day and always see something new." Her love of buildings and her dream of a perfect house of her own was what impelled her to window shop on streets lined with antiques shops long

Joe presents the Caffiéri bust of Benjamin Franklin to President Ford in the White House.

June and Joe present the Washington letter to Charles Wall of Mount Vernon.

June and Joe join Chief Justice Burger in the John Jay exhibit sponsored by the Supreme Court, 1978.

Virginia Archivist Louis Manarin accepts the Jefferson letter on behalf of Monticello.

before she persuaded Joe to go into one. "What I've always really wanted," she says, "is a beautiful house filled with beautiful things—and I knew I had to get Joe interested before I could achieve that." When asked what inspired her to buy this or that object, she says, "It just appealed to me. I *liked* it." Both Joe and Harold Sack credit June with an excellent eye and a real feeling for the objects she and Joe collect. Joe says that it took him years to realize that he should know they were going to buy something when June walked over and put her hand on it.

Unlike many leading collectors of both the present and past eras, Joe and June Hennage don't buy antiques they can't use in their house. If it's a better example of something they already have, they will trade the lesser piece in and buy the new one, but they don't store things or acquire them just to send them out again on loan. "Everything that we've put together," says Joe, "lives well together."

Shortly after discovering American antiques, Joe and June drove over to York, Pennsylvania, to visit the renowned Joe Kindig, Jr. Unfortunately, he died not long after that visit and their friendship never developed fully. Joe and June have since come to know and respect his son, Joe Kindig III, and have done a good deal of business with him. Because of their proximity to America's most fashionable furniture capital, both Kindigs specialized in Philadelphia furniture, as have the Hennages since the late sixties. Another Philadelphia-furniture expert with whom they've worked is Alan Miller, a restorer from Quakertown, Pennsylvania—of whom more later.

Although they've branched out and done business with a number of dealers—mainly in New York, but also in York, Pennsylvania, and in Philadelphia and Washington—June and Joe have bought the major part of their collection from Harold Sack. Harold has a history of working with customers to form outstand-

Joe Kindig, Jr. finally consented to set up the Charleston bed for June to look at it.

A Confederate $5.00 victory.

Joe Kindig III and June watch Alan Miller going over the Rhode Island kneehole desk.

June and Joe are inducted into the Raleigh Tavern Society by Colonial Williamsburg's Carl Humelsine, 1980.

ing collections, and he takes pride in that aspect of his job. Among those he's proudest of are the C. K. Davis, Lansdell Christie, and Mitchel Taradash collections, and his personal relationship with those collectors was of great importance to him. He's interested in early collectors and collections—the firm under his father, Israel Sack, formed some of the great early Boston collections—and he takes pleasure in reacquiring especially fine objects from estates or descendants and placing them in collections he's currently helping to build. Harold Sack's enthusiasm for the history of a fine object is catching, and Joe has come to share it. He's always pleased to get a piece from the Taradash, Christie, or Davis collections, or from an earlier one such as that of Mrs. J. Amory Haskell, Reginald Lewis, or George Horace Lorimer, dedicated antiques collector and editor of *The Saturday Evening Post* in the 1920s. Paying attention to previous collections forms a bond with other members of the American collecting fraternity.

From the sound of it, Harold had to work hard at his first sale to Joe. The object in question was a Connecticut high chest with a delicate verticality and elegant simplicity only rarely found. Joe recalls that the high chest was five times the price of other Connecticut high chests on the market at the time, but Harold maintained that its proportions were outstanding. Joe was traveling a good deal then, and he had occasion to compare prices in New England as well as in other New York shops. Finally, after months of discussing and negotiating, he agreed to buy the high chest. After they'd shaken hands, Harold said that some time in the distant future he'd be offering the Hennages two-and-a-half times what they'd just paid for their new piece.

Two years later Henry Maynard of the Wadsworth Atheneum called to ask if June and Joe would lend their high chest to an exhibition of Connecticut furniture. Joe agreed and offered to include a magnificent silver-handled, serpentine-fronted Connecticut chest of drawers in the loan. Maynard declined, saying he had plenty of chests, and Joe said, "I'll bet you $5.00 you'll be sorry you didn't take this one." Within ten days Maynard was back on the phone. "I owe you $5.00," he said, and asked if the Hennages would, after all, lend the serpentine chest of drawers.

The night the exhibition opened Harold Sack accosted Joe as he was admiring the displays and offered him a check for two-and-one-half times the price of the high chest. Joe told Harold he'd given the chest to June, and whether it was for sale or not was her

The Hennages stand with June's Connecticut chest of drawers while it is on view at the National Gallery.

decision. When Harold offered her the check, June asked, "Where will I find another one?" "You won't," he said, "because there isn't one." So June declined and kept the high chest. Before returning to the exhibit, Harold informed her that it wouldn't be too long before he'd be offering her *four* times the original price.

Shortly after this exchange, Joe was called to the podium to receive a Confederate five-dollar bill in mint condition, in payment of his bet with Henry Maynard. "You damn Yankees paid more for this than the $5.00 you owed me," he said, "but I'll always treasure it."

More than ten years later, at the opening of "In Praise of America," an exhibition at the National Gallery, Harold Sack once again offered June a check for the high chest—this time for twelve times the price she and Joe had paid. She asked Harold the same question, got the same reply, and the high chest once again remained in the Hennage collection.

* * *

The Hennages began their life together at a point when the American antiques world was reawakening after a long inactive period, and when Colonial Williamsburg was truly coming into its own as a museum of American political and domestic history. From almost the beginning of their marriage, Williamsburg was a special, magical world in which June and Joe could escape everyday worries, enjoy learning about and reliving American historical events, and dream of creating their own colonial home. When they built the house in Chevy Chase, they were able to incorporate many ideas from Williamsburg and to furnish it with reproductions from the Craft House.

As time went on and they began to collect antiques, June and Joe's sense of identity with Colonial Williamsburg became even stronger. Finally, in 1970, it dawned on them that Williamsburg meant more to them than anyplace else they knew or could think of. Why not use their expanding resources to help Colonial Williamsburg develop and prosper and to give others some of the pleasure they had enjoyed all these years? With that decision, Joe and June stepped out of the role of observers and into that of participants. They have been extremely generous in their support of a wide variety of projects since that time.

Now the Hennages have sold their red-brick house in Chevy Chase and are settled in a handsome house in the Georgian style, also of red brick, that they have recently completed in Williamsburg. The history of that project is related later. Their collection continues to grow, but always within the context of what Joe calls "the living collection"—that is, like the majority of the other collectors mentioned in this essay, they

acquire only what they can actually live with and use. Since antiques collecting first became popular, the most important motivation has been finding objects to furnish a house. That is what inspired the first Forumgoers to collect and that is what continues to inspire June and Joe. Fortunately, their new house is large enough to accommodate several more years' worth of collecting.

Franklin, in his *Autobiography,* said:

The next thing most like living one's life over again seems to be a recollection of that life, and to make that recollection as durable as possible by putting it down in writing.

In a sense, the Hennages are living the best of their lives over again, not by recalling it in writing, as Franklin did, but by spending each day in the place where they have always loved most to be. This book can serve for now as a recollection of June and Joe Hennages' lives, for there is much of them in it—much of their history, their hopes, and their accomplishments, not the least of which are the collection and the house they built to contain it.

Joe and June relax at the Williamsburg Lodge, 1951.

June and Joe examine the video equipment in the Hennage Auditorium with Charles Longsworth.

The Entrance Stairhall

When center-hall succeeded center-chimney houses in the early eighteenth century, space and light were among the new style's most pleasing features. Upon entering a Palladian-style house for the first time, the colonial visitor must have responded with delight to its capacious center hall and its clear and orderly plan of situating the main public rooms around the central entrance and passageway.

Entering the symmetrical front hall of Hennage House, today's visitor experiences that same sense of spaciousness and clarity of organization. A sensation of space and shifting light pervades the front hall—dim in the morning, filled with bars of sunlight in the afternoon. Splendid furniture, maps, and mirrors are ranged around and on the walls, conveying an immediate idea of the owners' collecting interests.

In the parlor, through the arch to the right, mahogany and yellow silk damask, polychrome Chinese porcelains, and English prints provide more visual evidence of the Hennages' taste, as does the library, seen through another archway straight ahead. Looking straight through the library past the furnishings to the mullioned window wall, the visitor first discovers scarlet geraniums on a gray stone terrace. From there steps lead down to a sizable lawn and, in the distance, the brick wall that separates the Hennages' property from the Williamsburg Inn's golf course. The ducks that live on the golf course pond pay no attention to the brick barrier, however; they often make themselves at home on the lawn and occasionally set up housekeeping there.

The entrance hall furniture introduces the collection's major themes. Each piece comes from an important colonial cabinetmaking center, and each is either an excellent example of a typical high-style form or a rare variant. Well-to-do citizens of the three leading pre-Revolutionary centers—Philadelphia, Boston, and New York—originally ordered the chests, chairs, looking glasses, and similar objects for their houses. Now, thanks to collectors like June and Joe Hennage, these handsome pieces can again be enjoyed in a domestic setting.

Immediately on the left of the hall is a handsome pair of walnut side chairs flanking a chest of drawers. Throughout the entire second half of the eighteenth century Pennsylvania patrons wanted, and chairmakers continued to supply, chairs representing all stages of the transition from Queen Anne to Chippendale. Like many examples made in the Philadelphia area, these two chairs retain stylistic elements of their Queen Anne predecessors. Their stiles are now straight and fluted rather than rounded and curved, their crest rails have taken on cupid's-bow scrolls, and their legs display acanthus carving and claw-and-ball feet, but the echo of the silhouetted shell in the crest rail and the outline of the vase-shape splat, now pierced, remain. Several other major collections contain chairs with very comparable features, including the Metropolitan Museum, whose arm chair appears to be from the same set as these two. A cherry example is said to have belonged to George Washington and to have been given by him to a member of the Morton family of Philadelphia.

In Philadelphia, low chests and bureau tables were popular dressing table forms, but a chest of drawers like this one sometimes served as a roomy and convenient alternative. Although similar chests had been in production since the Queen Anne period, examples of this kind with serpentine front, canted corners, and shaped bracket feet are characteristic of the Chippendale period. Many are fitted with the bail handles, as this one is, that came into fashion with the neoclassical period, lead- ing to the inference that such chests were still being produced late in the eighteenth century when the classi- cal taste succeeded the rococo for the most fashionable pieces. A particularly nice refinement of this mahogany example is the Chinese fretwork that replaces the usual reeded quarter-round pilasters in the canted corners. Also of note is the shaping of both top and feet to con- form to the lines of the facade. Occasionally, chests of this kind had top drawers fitted with boxes and compartments for dressing equip- ment or with writing slides; the present example has the latter amen- ity. Although chests of drawers similar in overall form and with canted corners and shaped feet have frequently been attributed to Jon- athan Gostelowe, it is now clear from similarities in design and con- struction that a number of cabinet- makers may have produced the form. This piece descended in the Stryker and Blackwell families of German- town, Pennsylvania.

The skill of the Philadelphia craftsman is highlighted in this bureau table. The bureau table, the eighteenth-century name for dressing tables of this form, became popular in England in the 1720s. By 1739 at least one Boston merchant owned an example, and by the 1760s cabinetmakers in principal American cities were making the specialized form for their fashionable customers. According to Nancy Goyne, bureau tables became especially popular in Philadelphia, where this example was made. One of the finest Philadelphia models, which for some reason are now extremely scarce, this elegant mahogany bureau exhibits restraint in carving, allowing the form's lines and proportions to make the decorative statement. The opulent pattern of the mahogany veneer on the drawer fronts adds warmth and liveliness.

In the short passageway leading from the front hall to the dining room hangs an architectural looking glass with a particularly lively phoenix rising from its pediment. This type of glass was nicknamed "tabernacle mirror" in England because it evolved from the niche, an architectural feature that held sacred images during the Renaissance. The placement of this looking glass is thus especially appropriate, as its reflection enlarges the feeling of an otherwise small space. In America, this type went by the name "Constitution" or "Martha Washington" glass. The latter name caught on perhaps as a result of Martha Washington's gift of such a looking glass to a congressman from Rensselaer County, New York.

Mr. and Mrs. Mitchel Taradash, who began collecting during the depths of the Depression, were former owners of this looking glass. Like the Hennage collection, the Taradash collection, formed first with Israel Sack and later with his three sons, began as furnishings for a home. They too eventually built a colonial-style house as a fitting backdrop for their antiques. The Sacks have written that the Taradashes built their collection as "the pioneers built our nation, with sacrifice, ingenuity and perseverance," and that "many of their great pieces were in major exhibits, publications and their home was shown in . . . 'Living with Antiques.'" For many years they were active in American antiques collecting circles and were well known attendees at shows and exhibitions.

As one enters the house a stunning pair of looking glasses catches the eye on either side of the opening to the library. Pairs of sophisticated antique objects in basically original condition are a great rarity. When the objects also have a well-documented history in distinguished colonial families, their desirability shoots sky high. These walnut looking glasses with carved and gilded ornament fall into both categories, having descended in the De Peyster and Rutgers families of New York and New Jersey. Their shape is primarily architectural, although abundant cartouches, scrolls, and acanthus leaves transform the earlier, more starkly linear version of this form into a compendium of rococo taste. One feels the presence of these glasses from anywhere in the hallway. Not only are they large and powerfully designed, with intricate highlighted surfaces, but they capture and transform the light in the room. It was surely an interest in controlling, directing, and even increasing light in otherwise dim buildings that caused looking glasses to be so highly valued in the eighteenth century.

Standing guard in the hallway just outside the parlor is this Philadelphia tall clock. Tall clocks, along with sofas and secretaries, were among the most highly prized furnishings of the colonial period. Usually created by two distinct specialists—the clockmaker and the cabinetmaker—these clocks were made for the wealthiest members of any community. As befitted their station, tall clocks often sat in a corner of the parlor, the most formal room in a colonial house.

The dial of this example is signed by Laurence Birnie, who advertised in the 1770s as a "watchmaker from Dublin, Ireland at Arch St. near Second" Street in Philadelphia. Its painted face incorporates a phase-of-the-moon dial and a second hand. The case, veneered with a rich, plummy mahogany, bears the marks of the finest type of Philadelphia furniture and must be the work of one of that city's most skilled cabinetmakers. Typical of Philadelphia cases, it features fluted quarter columns. The builder of the case remains unidentified, but he employed a number of decorative elements characteristic of fashionable Philadelphia Chippendale furniture: scrolled-leaf carving in the spandrels of the pediment, delicate pierced fretwork beneath the scrolls, and relief-carved rosettes on the scroll volutes.

Standing underneath one looking glass is the Philadelphia bureau table previously mentioned, while underneath the other glass is this Boston chest of drawers. Shaped facades with relatively little applied ornament enhanced the most fashionable case pieces made in Boston during the rococo period. The undulating lines of these blocked and bombé forms produced a very different result from that of the large, lavishly carved rectangular cases Philadelphia makers created. The rhythmic grace of this Boston chest illustrates the evolution from the spare linearity of late baroque Boston cases, with their simple rectangular shapes and serpentine legs and pediments, to the larger, heavier rococo examples, in which the serpentine line shapes the case itself. It took a skilled cabinetmaker to create the curved and blocked surfaces of such stylish pieces. The drawers of the most finely made examples follow the lines of the exterior, as these drawers do. Here, too, the bracket feet conform to the facade's serpentine shape.

Against the remaining wall in the entrance hall stands a side table that fits exactly into the space. Throughout the eighteenth century, as American builders adopted the Palladian style and new houses became larger, with symmetrically arranged interiors and facades, fashionable colonists began to order tables like this to stand in the evenly spaced piers between the windows of the parlor. The usual arrangement included a slab or sideboard table, as it was then called, and a sizable looking glass, which hung on the pier above the table top. Because marble was unharmed by heat and liquids, these made perfect serving tables, and this was their primary purpose. They were well suited to the mid-18th-century grand scale of entertaining.

According to Morrison Heckscher, these tables were usually placed in the parlor, where formal meals were customarily served until the advent of the separate dining room later in the century.

Thomas Chippendale published a design for a "Sideboard Table" in his *Gentleman and Cabinet-Maker's Director* that is clearly the source of this example: the square legs, simple Chinese brackets, and heavy molded top are the same in both the design and the Hennages' example.

This table was previously in the collection of Mr. and Mrs. Charles Gershenson of Detroit. Like the Hennages, they collected English antiques until, said Mrs. Gershenson, "I fell in love with a Philadelphia Queen Anne side chair." A whole new collection followed, of the same sorts of high-style American pieces the Hennages like.

Sideboard Table.

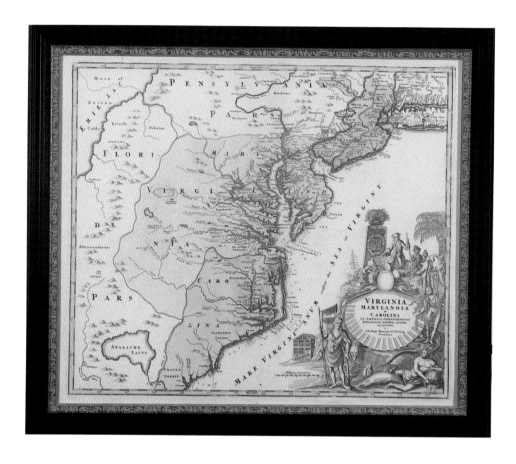

Visible from the entrance hall is a collection of period maps lining the stairway, most focusing on the Chesapeake region and neighboring colonies. They range from early representations of the New World through the American Revolution and offer a fascinating view of the changing perceptions of the American continent.

Although cartographer J. B. Homann's map was out of date geographically when it was published in Nuremberg, about 1735, its main purpose was to promote German immigration to Germanna, a new settlement to the west of Virginia's coastal communities. In the right-hand corner of the map are a peaceful depiction of friendly Indians, white settlers proudly indicating containers of gold and other kinds of wealth, and a palm tree suggesting a tropical paradise—a composite picture clearly meant to entice German citizens to the New World.

Until 1750, the Virginia House of Burgesses had ignored the need for an accurate map of Virginia. When they finally realized that plans for colonization and the need to resolve land disputes called for such a guide, they authorized Joshua Fry, surveyor and mathematician, and Peter Jefferson, surveyor and planter, to do the job—an almost unimaginably difficult one in the eighteenth century. The result, published in England in 1754 or 1755, charted the Virginia territory from the Atlantic coast to the Ohio River and was the most reliable map of the region published up to that time. This map is a French version published in Paris in 1755; it bears testimony to a considerable continental interest in

American affairs. The Hennages have both the English edition and this French copy.

The 1781 convergence of French and American land and naval forces on Yorktown, Virginia, represented one of the great feats of military planning in the eighteenth century. French cartographers carefully documented the march of Rochambeau's army from Connecticut to Virginia and its subsequent return to New England. Not only is the route shown, but each camp is noted.

The siege of Yorktown itself is depicted in this map by John Hills, a British engineer on the scene. He drew the original version of the map soon after the British surrendered on October 19, 1781. From the first shots fired at the ships in the harbor through the final defeat, the map offers a consolidated view of the events derived from on-the-spot observations. It was published by William Faden, London, in 1785, a fitting memorial to the end of the colonial era in Virginia.

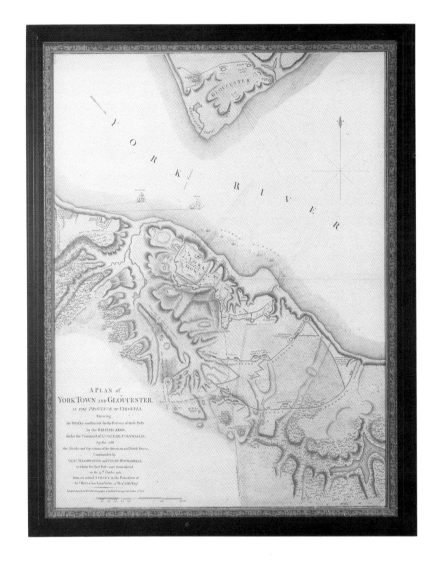

The Parlor

"This is a living collection," Joe Hennage always says about his antiques. He is referring to the fact that he and June have acquired their collection to live with, to furnish their home, not to store or put on long-term loan at a museum. Since they choose to live "informally with formal furniture," they have collected high-style American antiques of the eighteenth century. Philadelphia Chippendale pieces are their favorites, for the Hennages regard these as the most elegant and luxurious of all American colonial furnishings, made at the height of that city's prosperity and fashionableness.

Naturally, then, most of the parlor furniture is from Philadelphia and includes some of the most impressive forms made there. The magnificent Philadelphia furniture is complemented by selected pieces from other centers of high-style furniture such as Newport and Boston. The room conveys a feeling of elegance not only in its furniture, but also in the accessories that give a sense of unity. The draperies, the Chinese porcelains, the upholstery fabrics, all unite the individual parts into a pleasing whole.

Opposite the open doorway is this superbly carved mantel and over-mantel by Alan Miller. Just as many of the furnishings in this room are from Philadelphia, this mantel was modeled after those in stylish Georgian Philadelphia homes. Miller, a student of eighteenth-century Philadelphia designs and woodworking techniques whose studio is in Quakertown, Pennsylvania, took over a year to carve the fireplace wall. His design, while inspired by similar examples at Cliveden and the Powel House, is original. He worked with period tools and techniques to produce a work that is faithful to eighteenth-century ideals in spirit as well as in design. The cartouche at the top represents the Hennage coat of arms.

On the mantel is displayed a portion of June's collection of Chinese porcelain; the garniture, although not miniature, is of unusually small size. Its tobacco leaf decoration, popular in Europe throughout the entire second half of the eighteenth century, is found in five different combinations of color and design. The variation shown on this group was the most popular. Though it owed its origins to Chinese temple jars, the garniture, made up of five jars of two complementary shapes, was specially designed to decorate a Western fireplace mantel shelf, as here.

Another contributing element in the room, at times overshadowed by the many fine large pieces, is this Philadelphia clock. Clocks of all kinds were a luxury in the eighteenth century. Shelf clocks like this one were less expensive than tall clocks, however, because their works required only a third as much brass, their cases less mahogany, and they could be produced and sold much more rapidly than tall clocks. The Hennages' clock has an eight-day mechanism, which clockmakers developed toward the end of the eighteenth century. Mounted in an arched mahogany case with brass feet and fittings, it was signed on the dial by John Crowley of Philadelphia. Rising between a pair of global maps above the handsomely lettered and scrolled dial is a rare feature: a phase-of-the-moon dial combined with a shipping scene.

Two easy chairs and a serpentine-back sofa, the most comfortable seating forms of the colonial period, reinforce the ambience of leisure and luxury in the parlor. The two chairs have the strong, spirited curves that characterize the best Philadelphia easy chairs. The crisply carved legs are highlighted by shells on the knees, providing a focal point that complements the curves of the upper frame.

For some years before they began to collect furniture, June and Joe Hennage collected books and memorabilia relating to Benjamin Franklin, the father of the American printing industry and Joe's hero since boyhood. They were naturally delighted to be able to purchase the Franklin-Bache high chest, which descended in the family of Franklin's daughter, Sarah Bache. Whether it was actually owned first by Franklin or by his daughter is not known. It was used at Franklin Court, Benjamin and Deborah Franklin's home, where Sarah and her family lived with her mother after Franklin's death. Nearly all the characteristics of fashionable Philadelphia high chests may be seen on this example: a high scrolled pediment with applied shell and acanthus ornament on the scroll board, asymmetrical cartouche-shaped central finial, inset quarter columns on case fronts, acanthus-carved cabriole legs, claw-and-ball feet, and an elaborately scrolled skirt with a typical Philadelphia shell in its center. Harold Sack says that "even without the impressive history," this high chest belongs in the top echelon of Philadelphia case furniture.

Among the furniture that seems characteristically Philadelphia, the tilt top tea table certainly stands in the front rank. Because owning a special table and equipment for serving tea was so fashionable in the eighteenth century, tables, china, and silver were part of the parlor's permanent furnishings. In contemporary inventories, tea tables and their accoutrements are listed together; for example, "1 Tea Table with 6 China Cups & Saucers, and 1 Small Bowl" were cataloged "In the Blew

Lodging Room" at Stenton, one of the great colonial houses in Philadelphia.

This particular example, which descended in the family of William Dunn, founder of Dunnstown, Pennsylvania, is one of the Hennages' chief treasures. Its extremely fine carving and fluted column, a precursor of the flattened-ball column, make it unusually choice in both form and decoration.

Today, the curved outlines of Chinese porcelain teapot stands, saucers, and a spoon tray reinforce the undulating rhythm of the rim of this spectacular tea table. Made at various times and in various patterns from the third quarter of the eighteenth century into the nineteenth, these colorful dishes exemplify June Hennage's love of oriental porcelain colors and motifs.

The second of the two upholstered easy chairs in the parlor has a similar form but even more elaborate carving than the first. This choice example has the name "McClenachen"

inscribed in contemporary chalk on its back rail, the name of the family in which it descended. Upholstered furnishings were among the most expensive items an eighteenth-century householder could buy: the labor—joining, carving, and upholstering the frame—was only part of the cost. The fabrics, typically an imported damask, and often also a checked cotton or linen for a protective slipcover or "case," were what caused the price to escalate. That situation exists today as well be- cause of the high costs of both labor and luxury fabrics. The silk June has used throughout the room is a carefully reproduced eighteenth-century pattern.

Just as June Hennage takes great care to choose appropriate period fabrics for the chairs, Joe Hennage has tried for years to be certain that his chairs are accurately upholstered. He has conducted what Harold Sack calls "a vendetta" against upholsterers of easy chairs. Responding to research indicating that the stuffing tapered to nothing at the edges of easy-chair frames so that their elegant curves and planes would stand out sharply, Joe began to insist that his chairs be upholstered this way. It was an uphill battle, for upholsterers couldn't give up the habit of what Joe told them was overstuffing. On one occasion, he had the covering ripped off twice and begun anew before, on the third try, he got the result he wanted. The crisp outlines of these chairs testify to the effectiveness of his method.

The parlor's three looking glasses, all of either Philadelphia or English manufacture, are of the elaborate scrolled and gilded variety. Scrolled and carved looking glass frames complement the rococo carving of the furniture, and the glasses reflect what is already in the room, rather than introducing new subjects and colors.

This looking glass bears the bilingual labels (in both English and German) of John Elliott Sr., a cabinet- and looking glass maker who immigrated to Philadelphia from England in 1753. Elliott's labels state that he imported and resold English looking glasses and also repaired, reframed, and resilvered old glasses. This example is particularly important because of its unusually large size and surviving labels. The Elliott labels illustrated here, from a looking glass in the Colonial Williamsburg collection, are somewhat better preserved examples.

Flanking the parlor fireplace are two Philadelphia dressing tables displaying Chinese export porcelain, each paired with a looking glass. Although their prototypes were unmistakably English, the Philadelphia Chippendale chests that we call highboys and lowboys are distinctively American in form and ornament. Made as companion pieces, these practical pairs served for storage (high chests) and dressing tables (low chests) in eighteenth-century bedrooms. While solving the problem of storing clothes in a house without closets, these pieces added an additional dimension of elegance to the rooms they occupied. The elaborate carving, the highly figured woods, and the construction of furniture *en suite* clearly made a statement about the owner's aspirations and financial capabilities. The statement was neither unintentional nor misunderstood.

The dressing table to the left of the parlor fireplace is particularly fine. Representing the best of high-style Philadelphia taste, it exhibits a delicate Chinese fretwork band just below the top, quarter columns decorated with carved vines rather than the usual fluting, knees enriched with leafy brackets and graduated bellflower carving, and skillfully executed shell and acanthus ornament—one of Philadelphia's favorite combinations. Its small size and unusual number of beautifully planned carved details suggest that this table was made to order for a particularly discerning customer.

This architectural looking glass of English or Philadelphia origin is so similar to the looking glass on the opposite side of the fireplace as to seem to be its mate, but they are not a pair. Joe Kindig III, from whom the Hennages acquired this glass, notes that it is important "because of its extremely large size, having been the focal point in a monumentally scaled Georgian room in the Chippendale style." This looking glass and the Elliott glass now hang in a different Georgian room but continue to impress with their size and ornament. The Hennages have consciously chosen to collect looking glasses as their principal wall decoration. This decision is based not only on a fascination with the pieces themselves, but on a belief that they attract more attention to the other pieces in the room.

The dressing table placed to the right of the fireplace descended in the Varick and Stout families of New York. The carving on its knees, central lower drawer, and center skirt is richly conceived and vigorously executed, while that following the scrolling lines of the skirt itself is flatter—almost two dimensional. According to Harold Sack, there is a small group of such pieces with incised carving; perhaps their disparate decoration was applied in search of variety.

Standing prominently between the two parlor windows is this Philadelphia desk-and-bookcase. Hornor writes that in making the desk-and-bookcase and similar forms, "The craftsman was allowed to impress his individuality upon the product, while the patron could indulge his taste freely by ordering any carved elaboration to be seen in books of designs or elsewhere." Interiors of case pieces needed planning, too, and could be just as lavish as the exterior—or more so. The restrained exterior ornament of this example, for instance, gives way to extravagant blocked and serpentine lines on the inner tiers of drawers. Characteristic Philadelphia features include the broken scroll pediment ending in "sunflower" carvings, central rococo cartouche, inset quarter columns, and secret drawers.

Across the room from the desk-and-bookcase sits a finely upholstered American sofa. Perhaps the reason that so few wealthy Philadelphia families allowed themselves the luxury of a sofa like this one was, as William Hornor suggests, that "colonial dignity did not permit lounging in the presence of company." In fact, associations with the French court, and especially the female courtesans who were depicted reclining on sofas, may have proven distasteful to Americans. The sofa was, by all accounts, generally regarded during the period as a peculiarly female object thanks to these images. Other concerns undoubtedly centered on cost. Not only was the frame large and complex to make, but proper upholstery required vast amounts of fabric. In an age of hand looms and silk brought from China by sailing ship, it is hardly surprising that so few could afford such an elegant article as this. Whatever the reason, the form was never common, and examples such as this with sweeping serpentine crest rail and bold juxtaposition of angles and curves are prized rarities.

For some years, the Hennages had an English serpentine sofa in the parlor while they looked for an American sofa of the period. When this example finally came on the market, they bought it immediately and moved the English piece upstairs to stand between two Philadelphia chest-on-chests. Not only have they been able to keep a piece that they had come to cherish, but they have made it possible to compare the American version with its English counterpart.

"Old Joe Kindig's favorite chair," is how Joe Hennage often introduces his visitors to this piece. Like other similar chairs in the room, it retains the shells and vase-shaped splat outline of the Queen Anne period. Here, however, the lively crest rail ends in jauntily scrolled ears and the knees are carved with trailing acanthus leafage, giving it a definite Chippendale air. The dynamic forms of the arms, the crest rail, and the legs combine to give this chair a bold sense of movement in its overall design. It was the fine execution of the carving in combination with this design, however, that caused Albert Sack to rate it "best" in his *Fine Points of Furniture*. He noted that any number of Philadelphia chairs were made in this general shape, but few exhibit the graceful outline of this example. In form, proportion, and suitability of ornament, this chair represents the Philadelphia Chippendale style at its best. It is little wonder that Kindig, a man whose career was built on just such pieces, kept it for his own use.

Just in front of the sofa stands a rectangular tea table with tall, slender cabriole legs and pad feet, a form that began to appear in fashionable New England parlors in the mid-1700s. Often placed in the center of the room and kept set up with cups, saucers, and other tea drinking equipment, these elegant pieces proclaimed their owners' wealth and stylishness. Although definitely a Massachusetts form, this mahogany example came down in two Pennsylvania families. On its underside is an old paper label that relates the table's history of descent in the Shoemaker and Williams families. The writer also notes that at that time two high-backed walnut chairs "with loose hair covered seats" went with the table. The message ends, "I prize the set very much."

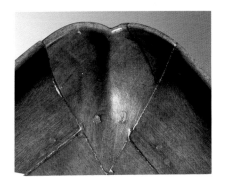

It seems fitting that in this room there should be a variety of comfortably upholstered seats—truly "easie" chairs. This fine Rhode Island example with a mellow old finish adds to the assortment of eighteenth-century leg and foot types visible throughout the room: the straight, square-sectioned, stop-fluted leg was particularly popular in Newport, Rhode Island. It belongs to a group of stop-fluted forms that Michael Moses calls "an important addition to the creative achievements of the Newport master craftsmen." So far as is known, none of these stop-fluted pieces was made before the Revolution; this chair was probably made between 1780 and 1795.

"Scollop'd" or "scollopt" top tea tables, now known as "piecrust" tables, were among Philadelphia's most distinctive and popular Chippendale forms, highly sought after both during the period and afterward, when people began to collect American antiques. This elegant piecrust table is descended from a line of distinguished collectors. Its first recorded collector/owner was Herman Clarke of Boston, an extremely discriminating gatherer of American antiques. Israel Sack's firm then acquired the table and sold it to Charles K. Davis, who was collecting fine American furnishings for his Fairfield, Connecticut, home. After Davis's death the Sacks obtained the table again and sold it to the Hennages.

The table is shown with a handsome neoclassical tea service sporting pineapple finials. The service is engraved with drapery swags and bears the script monogram *GP*, for Gertrude Polhemus of Staten Island. It was made about 1790 by Garret Schank of New York and bears his touchmark.

This Newport block-and-shell chest represents yet another approach to American Chippendale design: an undulating baroque facade is enriched simply but boldly with carved shells and shaped moldings. Joe and June Hennage waited many years to get this Rhode Island bureau, or kneehole desk. When the opportunity came, Joe assembled a group consisting of the dealer, an experienced and knowledgeable restorer, and himself to see that the piece was thoroughly "vetted" before he committed himself to the purchase. As it turned out, the piece

passed inspection with high marks for original condition, the only replacement being the set of brasses. Wallace Nutting had advertised the bureau, complete with its original brasses, in *The Magazine Antiques* in the 1920s, but they had somehow disappeared. The "witness marks" of the earlier brasses remained, however, and the Rhode Island School of Design had early hardware whose outlines exactly matched them. So new brasses were hand cast from those and now enhance the case.

Because the central section of the

shells is plain instead of being carved with a rosette, and because there are no fillets between the lobes of the shell, Newport furniture expert Michael Moses considers this an early example of the block-and-shell form. Another unusual feature is the small drawer beneath the central shell of the long top drawer: such a drawer is more typical of Massachusetts blocked chests than those of Rhode Island. The skirt of the little drawer does represent the painstaking craftsmanship of Rhode Island, however, in echoing the scrolling lines of the shell above it.

This set of six chairs has the same outlines as those of "Joe Kindig's" chair. "The whole sequence of Philadelphia-made chairs during this 'Golden Age' [1745-89] is in many ways equal to their London prototypes," wrote Hornor. Among the four characteristic Philadelphia chair patterns he mentions is this "strap-scrolled" variety, in which the standard Queen Anne vase-shaped splat is simply cut into interlacing scrolls. The shell in the crest rail is more elaborate than its Queen Anne predecessors, and there is lavish acanthus-leaf carving on the knees.

says, "It is apparent, however, that in looking glasses, as in so many other antiques, there are American styles, determined by the circumstances of colonial life, and that the examples used in America had a simplicity which brings them into harmony with contemporary forms of American furniture." The relatively simple architectural nature of this glass does indeed complement late colonial furniture, and Benjamin Ginsburg pointed out when he sold the Hennages the looking glass that its pierced shell was conceived "in the manner of the finest Philadelphia highboys."

Prominently displayed above the fireplace, this hand-colored print is one of the first items the visitor notices when entering the room. It is particularly appropriate for a setting that contains so much Philadelphia furniture. "An East Perspective View of the City of Philadelphia" was issued by Carington Bowles of London in 1778 as part of a series of views to be used "in the Diagonal Mirror, an Optical Pillar machine, or peep show." The machine referred to was a large, stereopticon-like affair designed to give the view under consideration an illusion of depth and three dimensionality. The rich gouache—rather than the more usual watercolor hues—adds to the effect of reality and enhances the print's visual appeal. This view was derived from an earlier study of Philadelphia by George Heap and is considered the most decorative of the reissues of Scull and Heap's East Prospect of 1754. It shows the steeples of the Statehouse, Christ Church, the Presbyterian Church, and the Dutch Calvinist Church.

This looking glass hanging above the Rhode Island bureau gives a chance to view the room from another perspective. Both Charles Montgomery and Helen Comstock, two highly astute American furniture scholars, have suggested that in all likelihood most sophisticated looking glasses were imported from England and sold here. Comstock

38. An East Perspective View of the CITY of PHILADELPHIA, in the PROVINCE of PENSYLVANIA, in NORTH AMERICA; taken from the JERSEY Shore.

1. Christ Church   3. Academy   5. Dutch Calvinist Church   7. Quaker Meeting House   9. Mulberry Street   11. Vine Street   13. Draw Bridge   The other Streets are not to be
2. State House   4. Presbyterian Church   6. The Court House   8. High Street Wharf   10. Sassafras Street   12. Chesnut Street   14. Corn Mill   seen from this point of Sight.

Printed for and Sold by BOWLES & CARVER, at their Map & Print Warehouse, N.º 69 in S.t Pauls Church Yard LONDON. Published as the Act directs.

The fireplace of the parlor is highlighted by a splendid pair of andirons adorning the hearth. Andirons of this design, with diagonally reeded vase-shaped turnings surmounted by faceted cubes and flame finials, are considered the ideal American Chippendale form. Perhaps this is because they complement furniture of that era so well, echoing themes such as claw-and-ball feet, C-scrolls, and twisted finials. Andirons in this same style recently set an Americana auction record in New York. The American Wing of the Metropolitan Museum has in its collections a pair of andirons of this pattern signed by Paul Revere, who worked in brass as well as silver.

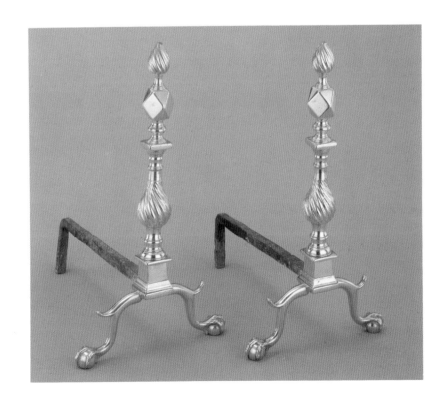

The Dining Room

Furnished with antiques from a greater variety of regions than most rooms in Hennage House, the dining room presents a survey of early Federal decorative arts. In its range of regions, it also illustrates another of the Hennages' goals: to obtain furniture from each of the original thirteen American states.

Although Chippendale furniture—particularly that made in Philadelphia—predominates in the collection, June and Joe chose early Federal, or neoclassical, pieces for the dining room because that was the period in which separate dining rooms became standard in fashionable houses. Furnishings specifically for dining were made in much greater numbers than ever before, so it was logical to focus on this period.

Against the wall opposite the fireplace stands a commodious English breakfront bookcase lined with beige silk and filled with important Chinese porcelain. The Hennages bought the breakfront early in their collecting career. It was one of a pair, but they persuaded the reluctant dealer to sell this piece singly. After completing this purchase, June and Joe went next door to an elegant antique porcelain shop, where they told the proprietor of the deal they had just made. They spent some time looking at porcelain, then said goodbye and departed. As they were walking away, the owner of the porcelain shop burst out of his door onto 57th Street and came running after them. "Young man," he called, "you're making a mistake. You ought to buy both breakfronts. Go back and get the other." Thinking this usually staid gentleman had lost his senses, Joe thanked him politely and walked on. It wasn't until he'd had a chance to mull over the dealer's advice that he changed his mind. And by then it was too late. Ever since he's been trying either to buy the other breakfront or to sell his to the other owner in order to bring the pair back together, but as yet he hasn't succeeded.

The crystal chandelier suspended from the ceiling was made in England between 1830 and 1840. When they found it, the Hennages loved it but were worried about the smoky gray color of the central crystal drop. Joe called the dealer to ask about the color. The dealer, Mr. Winston, replied that Joe could come in and select any comparable pendent in the shop. "But," he added, "that is the correct color for the period of the chandelier—the dark color tells you it's authentic." The drop remained and the Hennages later bought a similar, though smaller, chandelier, now installed in the parlor.

Appropriate for display in the dining room is the collection of Chinese ceramics in a variety of types and patterns. Westerners have long been fascinated with the products of the Orient, especially the porcelains. The Chinese invented and produced fine white-bodied wares centuries before the West, and the demand for these goods has been virtually insatiable. Americans, freed from the restrictions of their colonial status, certainly proved no exception to this trend of buying Chinese goods. Among the most sought-after China trade porcelains are those made for the American market and ornamented with designs, monograms, or arms that refer to a historic American event or

individual. If the piece carries an association with George Washington, it acquires extraordinary value. These three pieces are from Washington's own porcelain dinner service with blue and white Fitzhugh borders.

In the center of the two dinner plates and the berry dish (an extremely rare form) is the Angel of Fame holding a ribbon from which the emblem of the Society of the Cincinnati depends—a bald eagle. The Society was composed of officers who had fought during the American Revolution, with Washington serving as its president from its founding until his death in 1799.

June Hennage's interest in porcelains with American associations

doesn't stop with Washington. The plate with the narrow blue, rust, gold, and apricot borders is from a service Thomas Jefferson ordered from China. Its central motif is based on the Great Seal of the United States, an American eagle with sepia wings and a red, white, and blue shield on its chest. Surrounding the eagle's head are star-sprinkled clouds that serve as a background for a banner containing the words "E Pluribus Unum." The Chinese government presented a similar service to John C. Calhoun when he was vice president (1825-32).

The plate bordered by paintings of the harbor of Canton and the port of London bears the arms of the Lee family of England, from whom

Virginia's Colonel Richard Lee was directly descended. In the seventeenth and eighteenth centuries, Canton was the center of all European trade in China, since foreigners were not allowed onto the mainland. Silks, spices, teas, lacquers, and porcelains were assembled there to trade to Westerners, but even in Canton the "foreign devils" were allowed into only a tiny restricted area outside the walls of the city. With independence, American merchants established factories there.

The image of George Washington, commanding general of the Continental Army and first president of the United States, was a popular China trade motif during the last ten or fifteen years of the eighteenth century. After Washington's death in 1799, Americans continued to honor him by purchasing porcelain decorated with scenes of his beloved home, Mount Vernon. This plate featuring Mount Vernon in its center surrounded by a coral-red and gold border is a rare example of this type.

The pair of water bottles decorated with Chinese landscapes embodies a trend toward traditional oriental ornament that persisted in late eighteenth-century America despite the coincident taste for designs with nationalistic symbols. The vessels shown here bear the monogram of DeWitt and Maria Franklin Clinton, New Yorkers descended from Dutch and English families.

Typical of nineteenth-century Chinese porcelains made for Western consumption, the pair of dishes decorated with a bird pattern in iron-red and gilt is from a service made for Malcolm ("Bull") Smith of Smithtown, Long Island. One of the easiest ways to identify the original owner of a porcelain object is through a coat of arms, for the arms can quickly be traced to one specific person. The plate bearing the arms of John Morgan of Connecticut is a case in point.

From about 1770 until well into the nineteenth century the potters at Ching-tê-chên produced porcelains with a border now called—nobody knows why—Fitzhugh. Situated inland, far from the trading center of Canton, Ching-tê-chên was close to supplies of the clays from which the hard translucent Chinese porcelains are made. Father d'Entrecolles, an early visitor from the West, described the potteries at Ching-tê-chên in 1712: "In a Place encompass'd with Walls, they have built vast Pent-Houses [sheds], wherein appears abundance of Earthen Vessels, in rows one above another. Within this inclosure an infinite number of Workmen live and work, each having his particular Task." It was

reported, said Father d'Entrecolles, "that a Piece of China, by the time it is bak'd, passes the Hands of seventy Workmen."

The Fitzhugh border combines trelliswork, butterflies, flowers, and the Chinese key-fret design; an inner border is usually made up of four-part designs symbolizing the revered Chinese scholar. In pieces made for the American market, the center of the inner border is often filled with an eagle, coat of arms, monogram, or vignette instead of a mythical beast, as was traditional in China. Most examples of Fitzhugh porcelain made for the American market are blue and white, though several other colors were produced. June's collection contains a number

of the more uncommon colors such as the brown, or sepia, and rare canary yellow examples seen here.

The volume of porcelain imported into the newly established United States from China is staggering. Even though the potteries of England and the Continent were highly productive by the end of the eighteenth century, Chinese wares continued to top the list of quality ceramics, especially for dinner and tea services. Useful wares were not the only ceramics made in China for the American trade, however. Although plates and the like tended to feature designs chosen by Westerners, some popular objects with Chinese motifs and forms were imported. Miniatures made in China for the

Western market might have been intended for scaled down mantel shelves, but when massed together as are the garniture and animals in the dining room, they can fit anywhere. Chinese porcelain animals like these dogs-of-foo or temple lions and the pair of geese were the rage of Europe and ranged in size from miniatures the size of these to figures several feet high.

"The shapes and colors of Chinese porcelain appeal to me immensely," says June Hennage. The fine Kang-H'si vases on the dressing tables against the parlor fireplace wall, the wide variety of pieces on display in the dining room breakfront, and lamps and vases throughout the house represent her taste. Oriental rugs, used in all the downstairs rooms, glow with the same orangey reds and brilliant yellows that June likes so much in the porcelains. She has also adopted these colors for upholstery and window treatments—bright yellow predominates in the parlor and library and orange in the dining room.

This China trade porcelain tea service illustrates the high quality of work the Chinese could produce for the European markets. It is a remarkable blend of European forms with Chinese imagery. The service shows little evidence of use, particularly on the gilding, which is usually the first to wear. That is probably why so many of the pieces have survived, including the tea bottle and the cream jug, both with their covers, which are so frequently broken. The fact that the service is miniature, and presumably intended for the use of a child, makes its pristine condition seem nothing short of miraculous. Similar Chinese scenes on export ware have been found on many American archaeo-logical sites and were often copied on porcelain made both in England and on the Continent.

While the ceramics represent diverse foreign influences on the decorative arts of the early Federal period, the furniture of the dining room reflects the craftsmanship of the new republic. After the American Revolution, when New York became the biggest and most fashionable city in America, New York chair and cabinetmakers began turning out extremely elegant English-style neoclassical furniture. A number of New York makers produced the form of chair back seen here—a stylized draped vase holding three Prince of Wales feathers—taken from Pl. 36, No. 1, of Sheraton's *Cabinet-Maker and Upholsterer's Drawing Book* of 1794. These examples are very finely carved; the arm chairs have the added subtlety of a graceful leaf carved at the juncture of arm and rear stile.

Two prominent New York families, the Rikers and the Davenports, ordered the two apparently identical sets of chairs the Hennages own—perhaps from the same maker. The Riker family ordered the six side and two arm chairs about 1795 for their house on the East River at 75th Street; the chairs came down in the family. Apparently made for a house in the same part of the city, the Davenport set, which also descended in the family, is made up of nine side chairs.

The fireplace wall is the dominant architectural feature of the dining room, offering a highly appropriate setting for the Hennages' fine collection of American silver. The entire paneled wall was originally part of a 1760s house in Delaware. It had been removed early in this century and stored away by a New York dealer; its installation in Hennage House came after nearly fifty years in a warehouse.

Silver and Chinese porcelain collections are displayed in a handsome English breakfront and the two shell cupboards as well as on the table and sideboard. Colors from the porcelains—oranges, particularly—dictated the colors of carpet, upholstery, and window hangings. The cupboard interiors are painted a brilliant pink-orange, which June fell in love with in the Hewlitt Room of the American Wing at the Metropolitan Museum in New York many years ago.

Both June and Joe Hennage love to entertain and to share their home and their collection with their friends and collecting colleagues. "How can we have a living collection?" Joe asks. Then he answers, "By living with and enjoying and using the collection all at the same time." The table, which can be extended to seat sixteen, has made it possible for June and Joe to give sizable sit-down dinners in the dining room. Hosts and guests alike can experience the "living collection" by savoring the food, the company, and the collection throughout the evening.

The pair of mahogany dining tables, probably made in Boston around 1795, can be used either together or separately. They are especially unusual in their very narrow width once the leaves are dropped, making them convenient to store.

Elegantly showcased in the cupboards flanking the fireplace is silver that, like the furnishings, represents the workmanship of craftsmen from a variety of states. This tea set by John McMullin of Philadelphia epitomizes the early Federal style in its tall, slender, oval shape and shallow, shimmering engraving. Each piece bears the bright-cut monogram *SSJ* enclosed in a wreath of crossed branches; the owner of the initials remains unidentified. This bold statement of the newly fashionable neoclassical style was clearly made for a highly discriminating buyer, however.

An aspect of collecting antiques that interests Joe Hennage particularly is the associative one. For him, acquiring an object owned by a distinguished American family establishes a link with the colonial—or, particularly desirable in his eyes, the Revolutionary—period of our history. This superb rococo coffeepot of circa 1775, made by Richard Humphreys for the Taggart family of Pennsylvania, embodies the three requirements for the most desirable antiques: outstanding craftsmanship, its maker's mark, and a solid history of descent in an American family.

Josh B. Taggart, the last family member to own the pot, provided the following history: "The silver coffee pot by Richard Humphreys . . . had been in my family for several generations. It was left to me by my Great Aunt, Miss. Mary Taggart of Northumberland, Pennsylvania when she died about 1960. . . . I have in my possession correspondence from Miss. Mary in which she speaks of the . . . coffee pot as having belonged to her Grand-Mother. Just exactly who in the family first acquired the coffee pot I do not know. I do know, however, that it is an . . . original and that it was highly valued as an heirloom by all members of the Taggart family." One could hardly ask for more—a great pot, a great maker, and a great history.

Appropriate to the dining room display is this miniature portrait of one of the most famous American silversmiths—Paul Revere. Although perhaps best remembered as a patriot, he was a skilled craftsman whose career spanned the last half of the eighteenth century and the very early years of the nineteenth. During this period he worked as a silversmith, an engraver of copperplates, and as an entrepreneur in the copper industry. At the time of his death in 1818, he was at least as well known in Boston for his various commercial and manufacturing interests as for his patriotic activities. This miniature of Revere showing him late in life was painted by W. C. Russell in 1830 and resembles closely the 1813 portrait by Gilbert Stuart, now in the collection of the Museum of Fine Arts, Boston.

These five porringers represent a nice selection of the work of the finest Boston silversmiths of the late colonial period: Jesse Churchill, Jacob Hurd, Benjamin Burt, Daniel Henchman, and Paul Revere, the man at the top of every silver collector's "want list." Originally made to hold edibles such as berries or porridge, porringers were a sort of colonial sauce dish. In today's households, they serve many purposes both useful and decorative.

Baltimore was a city exploding in size, wealth, and vitality during the early Federal period. The new city was able to capitalize on its splendid location, taking advantage of its access to both the high seas and inland agricultural areas. Grain grown in central Maryland and western Pennsylvania could be brought by water to the city, where nearby waterpower permitted it to be ground into flour before its ex-port. Incoming goods followed the same path into the hinterlands. Though not established until the middle of the eighteenth century, Baltimore found itself the nexus of this new trade, and its prosperity knew no bounds. As the newly rich demanded more and more of the most fashionable goods, the city's craftsmen scrambled to fill the demand.

Silversmith Littleton Holland, for example, was active from 1802 until his death in 1847. Although a good deal of his silver survives, such as this six piece tea set, details of his origins and training remain unknown. The urn shapes, fluting, and bright-cut engraved ornament of these pieces are characteristic of earlier Federal silver, but their low, broad stance indicates that they were probably made after 1800, perhaps for a newly rich family.

Also from Baltimore were Andrew Ellicott Warner and his eldest brother, Thomas, both of whom almost certainly trained in their father's watchmaking and silversmithing workshop. The brothers were in partnership in Baltimore from 1805 until 1812, but both Thomas's covered jug and Andrew's salver date from periods when they were working alone. Andrew Ost-hoff, maker of the ladle, trained in Baltimore but moved west to pursue his fortunes after the War of 1812; the ladle bears touch marks used while he was working in Pittsburgh. The international tensions that culminated in the War of 1812 had proved an economic boon to Baltimore. As clashes between the French and the English became more frequent in the West Indies, the European trade in sugar became correspondingly fragmented. Baltimoreans were only too pleased to step in with their grain and other foodstuffs, and to become in turn a principal entrepôt in the sugar trade. The end of the war spelled the end of much of this trade, and it's not surprising to find men like Osthoff looking to the West to pursue their careers and better their fortunes.

The collection of silver displayed in the dining room includes pieces made in Philadelphia during the same period as the Hennages' prized Chippendale furniture—the middle third of the eighteenth century.

Much like its Johnny-come-lately sister city to the south, Philadelphia had earlier capitalized on its location. The Delaware River gave it access to the ocean, and the produce of all the rich farmlands of Pennsylvania funneled through the port. As with Baltimore a half century later, great fortunes were made and great houses were built. Furnishings in the latest fashion were highly acclaimed and much sought after.

While furniture responded to rococo fashions mainly by altering its decoration, silver took on actual rococo shapes. The reverse-pear form of the William Ball teapot, for example, is decidedly rococo in its curving and recurving lines. Its engraved designs are elaborately scrolled in the most fashionable European manner. The sauce boat by John David is one of a pair, and, like the shell ladle by the same maker, reflects clearly the aesthetic that was sweeping the city. The use of naturalistic decoration in combination with the fanciful curves of the scroll handles, for instance, results in a powerful statement. Earlier traditions and forms continued in use as well—the much simpler tankard was also made by John David.

Except for the cann fashioned by Benjamin Burt of Boston, the objects in this group were made by lesser-known New England silversmiths—proof that not all great work was done by the few craftsmen whose names happen to be familiar today. The sugar tongs were made by Thomas Arnold of Newport and are among the most graceful examples of this necessary accoutrement at the tea table. The diminutive pepper box, dated 1741, was made by John Blowers of Boston and is doubly charming with its attractive octagonal shape and commemorative inscription. Like so many pieces of American silver, it was a presentation piece executed in commemoration of an event, in this case a sad one. It was given to a loving aunt as a memorial to her nephew who "died upon the Coast of Africa." We may never know for sure, but he was apparently a victim of the very trade that enabled the purchase of such fashionable and expensive furnishings. The covered tankard is the work of Nathaniel Morse of Boston, a classic of its form. The Benjamin Burt cann, with its neoclassical engraved swags, is clearly later than the other pieces. It bears the initials of Forman Chessman, a shipbuilder, and his wife, the former Ann Cummings.

Boston, Philadelphia, New York, Rhode Island, and Baltimore are all well represented in this collection of silver. The Hennages were pleased to be able to purchase this set of four salts because it added one more area to this list — Alexandria, Virginia. While Virginia did not have as many famous silversmiths as the other cities mentioned, Alexandria was one of its chief centers of silver production in this period.

Like Baltimore and Norfolk, Alexandria flourished later than the more established colonial cities. Also like these coastal cities, its prosperity was based on its ability to foster an international trade in the agricultural products of its inland regions. This commercial success, linked with the notoriety that attended the relocation of the nation's capital to the new Federal city across the Potomac, led to the development of a community of craftsmen able to fulfill the demands of a new generation of patrons. Many of their products approached in sophistication those that came from the more firmly entrenched cultural centers.

John Adam, Sr., a prominent Alexandria silversmith, fashioned this set of four silver gilt-lined salts in the 1790s. They are unusual both in their design, having hemispherical bowls supported on short pedestal bases of circular plan, and in the survival of a set of such number. John Adam, Sr., and later his son, also used this form of base for tea and coffee wares.

Recent additions to the collection of Philadelphia silver have included this elegant oval tea caddy of about 1795 by Joseph Richardson, Jr., and a tea caddy spoon of similar date by John David. Such oval caddies supplanted the smaller tea canister in the years after the Revolution. Distinctive neoclassical features include its plain oval form, urn-shaped finial, and decorative engraving with a laurel wreath for its owner's cipher. The use of beading or pearling, seen in the finial and at the rim and base of the body, was especially popular with Philadelphia artisans and their clients. Tea caddy spoons such as this handsome example, its handle bordered with bright-cut engraving and its bowl of shell form, were introduced at this time for use with caddies.

The cipher *FC* engraved within the laurel wreath of the caddy may be for a member of the Clifford family, for the underside is later inscribed "H. Morris to A. Clifford." This piece was formerly in the collection of May and Howard Joynt, friends of the Hennages from Alexandria, Virginia.

While the silver collection focuses on American pieces, one superb example represents some of the best English craftsmanship in the period just before the Revolution. This splendid epergne provides a dazzling focal point to the dining room at Hennage House. Epergnes, their baskets and saucers laden with fruit and sweetmeats, came into their own during the third quarter of the eighteenth century. Through the extravagant use of piercing and slender cast elements of scrolled and naturalistic design, they achieved the important rococo aims of lightness and grace.

When the Hennages first acquired their London epergne of 1768/9, marked *TP* and credited to Thomas Powell, they asked John Graham, then chief curator at Colonial Williamsburg, to look at it. Upon seeing the piece, Graham immediately said, "That's not Powell, that's Pitts!" Then, to relieve Joe's visible consternation, Graham continued, "But Pitts is really much better anyway, because he was a leading silversmith in eighteenth-century London who specialized in epergnes." Thomas Pitts, in fact, even supplied epergnes within the London silver trade for retail by other firms.

A fitting reflection of the graceful rococo scrolls of the epergne is offered by the pair of English giltwood wall brackets. As with so many other examples of the rococo, their powerful presence is relieved to a large degree by the fanciful curves and open piercing. Their demeanor on the wall is strong but not overbearing.

Objects that can be associated with Revolutionary heroes and events have been of primary interest to collectors since the first eccentric men and women began to gather American antiques in the mid-nineteenth century. Those first collectors were usually more interested in the associations than the aesthetic qualities of their things, however, and it wasn't until the 1880s and 1890s that a few artistically inclined collectors began to unite the two interests. By now the pendulum has swung, and today aesthetic considerations often take precedence over associative ones. These handsomely formed andirons are both stylish and engraved with the Revolutionary slogan "Liberty or Death" and a liberty cap, symbol of freedom. Their patriotic motifs recall our nation's newly won independence.

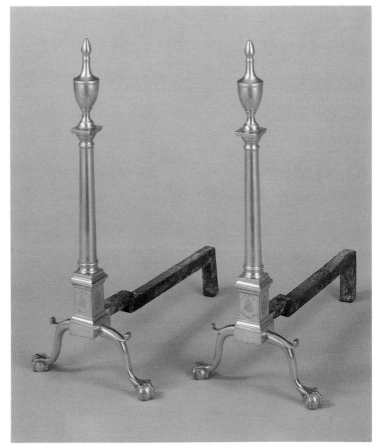

More than any other American city of the time, Baltimore strove to stay abreast of world fashions. Not only were its merchants and traders in regular contact with the major metropolitan centers of England and the Continent, but the city played host to a flood of immigrants as well. Many opportunistic craftsmen sought out the less rigid society of the new country, and they brought with them an awareness of the latest fashions. They came seeking fortunes, they came fleeing revolutions, but in each case their presence was felt.

Baltimore cabinetmaking is represented in the dining room by this ample sideboard, an example of that city's fashionable neoclassical fur-

niture. Here lively veneers in oval and rectangular shapes combine with bellflower inlays and small ovals enclosing unusual bulblike forms to create a symmetrical, yet spirited, facade. An almost identical example is in the Baltimore Museum of Art, where it is considered among the finest of the forms produced in Baltimore between 1790 and 1815.

Hanging above the sideboard and presenting an intriguing view of the room is a splendid convex gilt-framed mirror. Made from about 1800 onward, round convex glasses like this were the first to be called "mirrors," according to Thomas Sheraton's 1803 *Cabinet Dictionary*. Their round or oval frames were more difficult to make "than

any other looking-glass frames of the Federal period. Probably not half a dozen shops in the whole country could have produced them," wrote Charles Montgomery. It is possible, of course, that this mirror is not American but English, for dealers in looking glasses and mirrors usually advertised that they sold imported examples as well as making new ones and repairing old or damaged ones. Whether native or foreign, however, this mirror is extremely fine, with elegantly scrolling candle arms, engaging dolphins and a vigorously modeled eagle. Of special interest is the two-toned gold leaf used on the dolphins, a feature that became evident only when the gilding was cleaned and restored.

Across the room from the convex mirror hangs a more conventional, but nonetheless striking, looking glass. The rectangular form, applied pilasters with corinthian columns, balls under the cornice, and eagle finial of this glass are typical of the early Federal period. The delicately shaped cone finials that flank the eagle are unusual, however, and the quality of the work is superior throughout. The addition of a *verre églomisé* portrait of Mount Vernon makes this New York glass a collector's dream.

Following Washington's death, Mount Vernon was widely recognized as symbolic of the much memorialized hero. Beyond its associations with Washington, however, it represented the agrarian basis of the new republic. Home to the American Cincinnatus, it stood as symbol of all that was good in the reliance of an independent people on the land, a reliance that men like Thomas Jefferson both recognized and encouraged. Joe says simply, "When I saw Mount Vernon— Wow!"

Below this looking glass sits Rhode Island's contribution to the room. Newport's Golden Age occurred during the Queen Anne and Chippendale periods, when the great block-and-shell pieces were made. Though this serpentine chest of drawers was made late in the eighteenth century, it exhibits the energy and style of earlier case pieces. It is similar in many ways to an example of 1798-1806 labeled by Holmes Weaver of Newport, which is illustrated in Moses's book on Newport furniture.

The Library

June's personal attraction to Chinese colors and objects has resulted in a theme that is visible throughout the house—that of mixing oriental and American colonial objects. In the library, oriental art in porcelain and woven form joins with an eighteenth-century Chinese Chippendale mantelpiece from England in an especially harmonious interplay. On the mantel and elsewhere in the room are small Chinese porcelain animals and vases in glowing colors. As in all other areas of her house, June has chosen one or two basic colors for the upholstery—canary yellow spiced with orange here—and has added other color accents through the use of oriental rugs and Chinese porcelains. In order to display their furniture to greatest advantage, the Hennages have chosen to paint their walls rather than to paper them. Trim in the library is painted a green based on that used in Colonial Williamsburg's Raleigh Tavern. Because they weren't trying to use an exact eighteenth-century color, June and Joe just had the painter mix the paint until the shade pleased them.

The furnishings in this room complement the furnishing scheme in the rest of the house. Although several pieces here are from Philadelphia, the Hennages' preferred furniture center, there are also a number of objects from Boston and Newport. Their use together facilitates comparisons between Pennsylvania and New England on the one hand, and within the New England area on the other. The whole provides a suitable setting for an enviable collection of books on art, architecture, and decorative objects, including many volumes that are rare and difficult to find.

June's belief that "Impressionist paintings and American antiques look wonderful together" is borne out by her decoration of this room. The painting above the mantel, a colorful impressionistic vase and flower arrangement set against a dark background, embodies the same sort of contrast as that created by bright yellow and orange upholstery on dark mahogany furniture. The painting's Chinese flavor is heightened by the crossetted frame around it. Below, on the mantel shelf, June has placed Chinese vases filled with yellow and orange flowers whose shapes and colors echo those of the painted ones.

If seated or standing in the right place in the room, one can view these Chinese elements in the reflection of this elegantly ornamented Western looking glass. Three distinct stylistic points of view come together in this one piece. Its rectangular shape and broken-scroll pediment with rosettes ending in leafy scrolls are characteristically architectural, based on designs for doorways and chimneypieces that became fashionable in America about 1750. Its leaf-and-flower pendents, asymmetrical phoenix finial, and scrolled bottom pay homage to the rococo style fashionable in America between 1760 and 1790. Finally, its gilt-tracery decoration of leaves and palm sprays belongs to the delicately decorative neoclassical period of the late eighteenth century.

Besides representing an interesting stylistic mix, this glass bears the paper label of Hosea Dugliss of New York. The label reads: "Hosea Dugliss,/ Looking Glass/ Manufacturer,/ 21 Chatham Row,/ Between Ann Street and/ the Park Theater,/ New York." Because Dugliss appears in the New York City directories for the first time in 1818, some years after this style of looking glass had gone out of fashion, it is likely that he simply repaired the glass and added his label at that time. He appears to have used this label between 1832 and 1848. Also on the reverse of the looking glass is an inscription in ink. The letter "L" encloses a "G R" in its upper loop and an unintelligible letter in its lower loop. Underneath the bottom stroke of the L is the date "August 1770 [or possibly 1790?]."

Excellent proportions, design, and craftsmanship distinguish this Philadelphia armchair, whose splat pattern was popular both in England and the colonies. Hornor shows a number of nearly identical splats on Philadelphia chairs, and Jobe and Kaye illustrate two in this exact pattern—one from a set ordered in London by a wealthy New Hampshire merchant to furnish his new house in Portsmouth, and the other from a set of copies the same merchant ordered from a local Portsmouth craftsman, providing us with proof that designs traveled across the ocean in a number of different ways.

In commenting on the Yale Art Gallery's four Philadelphia examples with this splat pattern, Kane points out that they are based on, but are not exact copies of, Plate X of Chippendale's *Director* of 1762. Another example, at the Henry Ford Museum, has Marlborough legs like this chair, but they are decorated with Chinese fretwork while these are plain except for the C-scroll bracket that connects the legs to the front seat rail.

While the library is furnished primarily with chairs and tables at which to sit and enjoy the books, there is one case piece that stands out because of its form and beauty.

Blockfront furniture, particularly popular in pre-Revolutionary New England, was made in a variety of forms that include the dressing table, desk, desk-and-bookcase, and chest of drawers. Once in the Taradash collection, the Hennages' very fine chest was made between 1760 and 1780 in Boston, where the first documented American blockfront case piece was created in 1738. Among this example's refined features are rounded blocking and four delicately delineated claw-and-ball feet. Also notable is the fact that the chest retains its original pine-tree brasses and side carrying handles.

Unlike most fashionable forms, which were relegated to attic, barn, or storeroom when their popularity declined, "No furniture has been more highly prized than the sophisticated blockfront furniture of Boston and Newport," write Jobe and Kaye in *New England Furniture.* "Consequently, blockfronts tend to survive, and museum collections display so many that it is hard to believe that these were special objects, afforded only by the wealthy."

New Englanders' penchant for blocked furniture is also seen in this beautifully proportioned and carved card table that descended in the Larkin family of Newburyport, Massachusetts. Tables of this sort, with projecting square corners flanking a concave central block, long, slender legs, and delicately carved claw-and-ball feet, were made for numerous well-to-do families in Massachusetts and Rhode Island. Some were plain, relying entirely on bal-

ance and harmony of form for their effect, while fewer were enriched with crisp carving, as this one is. The addition of carved details, here acanthus and C-scrolls, and other niceties such as the drawer in this example naturally increased the price to the original customer—and today increases the table's appeal to collectors. The design of this table is but one of many variations in the card table form. The considerable diversity in design and construction

of surviving examples suggests the widespread popularity of the card table, and of gambling in general. Then, as now, cards often provided a social common ground.

Just as with so many pieces in the dining room, the andirons in the library provide a link with a distinguished family of the colonial period. About fifteen years ago, the Hennages told a Philadelphia dealer they were in the market for andirons of the highest quality. Later, jus before the University Hospital show opened, Joe and June were delighted to receive a call from the dealer saying he had a pair originally owned by Colonel Tench Tilghman, aide-de-camp and military secretary to General Washington during the Revolution. In gratitude for his faithful service, Washington had honored Tilghman by asking him to take the news of the surrender at Yorktown to the Continental Congress in Philadelphia.

Joe immediately told the dealer to hold the andirons until he and June got to the opening. When they arrived and spotted the Tilghman set, Joe said immediately, "I'll take them." "Fine," said the dealer, and named a four digit price. Joe was amazed. "Where's the pair of andirons that's ever sold for more than eight or nine hundred dollars?" he demanded. Pointing out that this wasn't just any pair of andirons, the dealer stated firmly that unless he got his price, he was going to keep them. He had another pair, he said, for considerably less money, and the Hennages were welcome to buy those instead. With very little more to-do, Joe and June bought both pairs and have lived with them happily ever since.

The Tilghman andirons, seen here, have square bases with bright-cut engraved ornament and urn-shaped columns with lemon finials in the neoclassical style of the late eighteenth century; their claw-and-ball feet remain in the style of the previous rococo period.

during the 1770s as the situation between the colonists and the British worsened.

In September 1774, then Colonel Danielson was in Concord as a delegate to the provincial congress. In answer to the alarm of April 19, 1775, he led a regiment of Minutemen on the march to Lexington. Later that year he was appointed colonel in the Massachusetts Army encamped at Roxbury during the siege of Boston. In 1777, he became brigadier general of six volunteer Massachusetts militia companies called out to reinforce the army at Fort Ticonderoga. Subsequently, he headed a secret expedition and was appointed major general on May 10, 1781. After the war, the general was a member of the convention that framed the Massachusetts state constitution.

General Danielson's easy or "wing cheek" chair, as it was known in the family, belongs to a group of such chairs that share a number of characteristics. They are vertically oriented with bowed crest and front seat rail, have straight-sided serpentine wings that flow into canted cone-shape armrests, and block-and-ring-turned stretchers joined to cabriole front legs and squared, outsplayed back legs. There is one significant difference in appearance between this and many other examples in the group: it has claw-and-ball, rather than pad, feet. Yet, as Heckscher reminds us, "The traditional distinction between Queen Anne and Chippendale is not valid for the American easy-chair form. Rather...they must be lumped together as 'cabriole chairs.'"

Like the New York looking glass, this arm chair brings together elements from a variety of styles. Similar to the splat-back chairs in the parlor, this example is even closer to its Queen Anne predecessors. While its cupid's-bow crest rail, low squarish back and seat, and claw-and-ball feet are Chippendale hallmarks, its simple, uncarved framework and shell decoration recall the previous style. Although it has now been converted, this originally served as a potty chair. It is another piece that was once owned by a distinguished earlier collector—in this case, Albert Whittier of Boston.

Like the Tilghman andirons, this easy chair was made for an American patriot. General Timothy Danielson of Brimfield, Massachusetts, ordered the chair from a Boston maker during the pre-Revolutionary period, probably between 1760 and 1770. He had many occasions to be in and around Boston

Among the chairs in the library is this Philadelphia armchair, a chair that Joe was delighted to acquire. On one recent occasion when he was showing it to guests, he called it "the King's chair" because, he said, "of its size and proportions."

It belongs to a small group of upholstered-back open-arm chairs with Marlborough legs made during the Chippendale era by one or more of Philadelphia's most skilled chairmakers. Of such chairs Hornor writes, "side by side with the carved-splat chairs of the Cabriole period there were the group of upholstered-back chairs, which are recognized for their urbanity and desired because of their comfort. . . . Until the end of the Chippendale influence, these products were of a much higher quality than the average chair." Some chairs in the group have fret carving or panels with pendent bead and flower designs on their Marlborough legs, but whether elaborate or more simply ornamented with decorative astragal molding, as this example is, all are based on Pl. XIX of Chippendale's 1762 *Director*. The reel and bead molding on the arms was used by several of the finer Philadelphia shops. It lends distinction to a form that might otherwise appear somewhat spartan by the standards of the period.

Flanking the sofa in the library is a handsome pair of tables. Pembroke tables, made in Philadelphia at least as early as the 1770s, were useful, movable forms for dining or other occasional use whose small drop leaves made them doubly practical. Sheraton later stated that the form was named for the lady who ordered the first one "and who probably gave the first idea of such a table to the workmen." Though unornamented except for their finely figured mahogany tops and molded legs, these tables are, according to Harold Sack, "of the highest quality of design and material and . . . most unusual in having survived as a pair."

Charleston Bed and Sitting Rooms

Pieces from several leading eighteenth-century furniture centers occupy the Charleston bed and sitting rooms, which are located just off the center hall in a corner behind the parlor, next to the library. Its convenient location makes this little suite, complete with bathroom, useful for guests to rest and freshen up.

Like the other downstairs rooms, prominent Georgian moldings and white plaster walls serve as a backdrop for the antiques. Here the trim color is mustard yellow, which accords well with the dainty flowered silk window and bed hangings, chosen because the scale of the pattern corresponds to that of the delicate leaf patterns carved on the posts at the foot of the bed.

Besides Philadelphia, the city whose cabinetwork is best exempli-

fied in the Hennage collection, and Newport, from which there are also many examples, Connecticut and Charleston, South Carolina, are represented in the bedroom. It was the latter city that produced the handsome mahogany bedstead that gives the room its name.

The first antique the Hennages bought from the firm of Israel Sack was this high chest. For collectors who had been focusing on English high-style pieces, it was quite a leap to acquire a provincial American high chest. After the sophistication and subtlety of old-world furniture, the verticality, simplicity, and delicacy of this piece must have seemed refreshingly direct, even quintessentially American. Of it, Harold Sack says, "It has the classic majesty of the superlatively formed Massachusetts highboys characteristic of the major seaport centers of Boston, Salem, and Newport." This example, however, was made in Connecticut, where, instead of the more direct sources of new fashions available in large cities, cabinetmakers often had to rely on word of mouth and examples of pieces made in fashionable urban centers that made their way into town. The result was furniture that frequently borrowed from diverse sources that included Massachusetts, Rhode Island, New York, and Pennsylvania.

Joe Hennage feels that his high chest's greatness comes from its proportions, the rhythm of its silhouette, and its graceful cabriole legs and scalloped apron. It belongs to what John Kirk has called "the elegant style, which depends for its design upon superb proportions and the movement and interaction of beautifully shaped curves," rather than the complicated, sometimes quirky designs of many other pieces of Connecticut furniture.

Particularly appropriate to a bedroom is a dressing table. Fitted dressing tables were rare in America in the eighteenth century, perhaps because most people preferred a skirted dressing table and chose to invest their money in costly fabric rather than in cabinetmaking. (This suggestion is made by Monkhouse and Michie, who quote an early correspondent on the practice of fitting dressing tables with muslin skirts "made full and deep . . . descending to the floor.")

This delicately designed mahogany example is from Rhode Island, and the slender width and arrangement of its drawers are very similar to those of dressing tables with scrolled skirts carved with the familiar serpentine Newport shell. The square-section tapering legs suggest a date late in the century when this type came into fashion.

Among the legendary figures in the world of American antiques, Joe Kindig, Jr., stands out. Known to his admirers and detractors alike as

"the first hippy," he did business with long hair, a luxuriant beard, bare feet, and sandals. Along with only a handful of other American antiques dealers, he was a legend during his lifetime, and collectors all over the country venerated his knowledge of fine antique furniture and Kentucky rifles. "If he liked you and thought you were seriously interested," said one notable collector recently, "Joe Kindig would go out of his way to talk to you and share his knowledge. But if he didn't—look out!" This is the kind of reputation that often puts off novice collectors, keeping them out of the shops—and the line of fire—of such dealers.

June and Joe Hennage ventured into Joe Kindig's York, Pennsylvania, shop toward the end of his life, and June says "the minute we met, we liked each other. There was a kind of natural understanding between us." Kindig no doubt admired June's eye for quality and her innate ability to appreciate interesting and artistic objects. On their second visit, the Hennages spotted a Charleston bedstead lying disassembled in a corner of Kindig's warehouse. They inquired about it and Joe told them it was the finest bedstead available anywhere. Winterthur had one like it, he said, and they should go up to have a look at it before deciding whether or not to buy his. During the Hennages' third visit, after they had visited Winterthur to study the four-post bed there, June asked Kindig to set the bed up. At first he said, "we never do that," but June was persuasive and in a little while he had the bed assembled. They bought it and it now serves as the focal point in this downstairs suite, named for its place of origin.

100

The bed's foot posts, carved in the stylized leaf patterns and ornamented with the stringing that are characteristic of South Carolina, make it a special piece. Kindig wrote that they were "unusually beautiful[ly] proportioned . . . finely reeded, carved, and inlaid."

Reflecting another, later style, is this elegant yet decidedly capacious desk with tambour section, which belongs to a sizable group of tambour desks made in New England during the Federal period. Although the best-known examples have only two drawers instead of four and are mounted on slender, tapering legs, this is a practical variant that provides much more drawer space than its smaller relation. The refined decoration of the piece, and its very delicate veneers, gave special challenges to the cabinetmaker. The tambour doors, for instance, are made of individual strips of wood mounted on a canvas backing, enabling them to slide around the side corners. Precise, highly skilled craftsmanship and veneers of swirling flame-grained satinwood lift this desk far above the ordinary. It sits in a small light-filled sitting room just off the Charleston bedroom.

Like many other objects in the Hennage collection, this desk has an enviable pedigree, having been owned by two discriminating early collectors of American antiques. The first was Herman Clarke, whom Harold Sack describes as "a truly great connoisseur of Americana." He lived in Boston, where he amassed a superb collection of both furniture and silver—often with the help of Israel Sack, whose firm was established there before it moved down to New York. During the

Depression Clarke became so despondent about America's future that he sold many of his most valuable pieces. He was afraid if he didn't sell them for cash while there was still some around, the economy would worsen and no one would be able to buy them.

Charles K. Davis, the desk's subsequent owner, was for many years head of Remington Arms, makers of handguns and long arms since 1816. He was a production genius who masterminded the American effort to resupply the British with ammunition after the evacuation of Dunkirk in 1940. In his leisure hours, Davis collected antiques of the highest quality for his home in

Fairfield, Connecticut. As was typical of many other early American antiques enthusiasts, his collection represented the entire range of American styles from the seventeenth century to the nineteenth.

This little tea table or candlestand from Philadelphia exhibits the usual support for tripod tables: a column resting on a ball. Hornor notes that cabinetmakers could either buy ready-made parts for such tables or they could send their own wood out to a turner, who would then shape pillars and colonnettes and round the top boards—an instance of production-line manufacture at an earlier period than we usually suppose.

A sideboard, with a full complement of silver, glass, and ceramics, was a necessary feature of the proper dining room by the end of the 18th century. It was the room's vital focal point.

This captivating little sideboard is an unusual addition to the Hennage collection, for while it is very stylish, it is not *high* style in an urban sense. June says that she had her eye on it for years before she and Joe finally got it; when they were considering it some time ago, another customer bought it first and they had to wait until it came on the market again. The sideboard's charm results from its small size—always an attraction for June—its correspondingly delicate proportions, and its black- and light-wood inlays, which give it a feeling of lightness and gaiety. The mahogany veneer on drawer and door fronts is beautifully matched and is crossbanded with curly maple. Its place of origin has not yet been determined exactly, as it seems to have characteristics of New Hampshire, northeastern Massachusetts, and Rhode Island.

The Gothic-backed chairs shown here, of a set of six, belong to a large family of similarly patterned Philadelphia side chairs, but they are among the plainest examples. The flat, uncarved splat and simple square legs create a pleasing, almost stencilled, effect.

In explaining the sources of inspiration for the style he immortalized in *The Gentleman and Cabinet-Makers Director,* first published in 1754, Thomas Chippendale named the Gothic along with the Chinese and rococo. "Our home, our beds, our bookcases and our couches were all copied from some parts or other of our old cathedrals," wrote a contemporary London publication to indicate the pervasiveness of Gothic designs. Philadelphians were similarly taken with the style, and Hornor states that "If there is any single [chair] back which may be said to have been the criterion of the Philadelphia-Chippendale makers, it is the Gothic."

This diminutive chest is the kind of thing June Hennage especially likes: a beautifully planned and executed formal design that is a little unusual. The atypical feature is the chest's small size, for June is drawn to miniatures. In all other respects it is characteristic of its time and place—the Chippendale period in Philadelphia. Its inset fluted quarter columns, top notched at the corners, boldly curved ogee bracket feet, and use of walnut for a high-style form in the Chippendale period are all typical of Philadelphia.

Flexibility and portability were hallmarks of eighteenth century furniture, as they are today. Space was at a premium, and furniture frequently had to be moved around in a room, a fact that often dictated the form of the individual piece. Philadelphia furniture shops produced a variety of table types with straight molded legs and skirts edged with refined gadrooning. In fact, the most carefully and delicately carved American gadrooning was produced in Philadelphia, as exemplified by the edging of the skirt of this small drop-leaf table. Although this feature has often been associated with the work of Thomas Affleck, Kindig points out that it must have been produced in other shops as well. It is clear that this little table is the work of one of Philadelphia's finest shops.

An unusual feature of this piece is the gadrooning extending the entire width of the skirt instead of only from the inside edge of one leg to the inside edge of the leg opposite. This is especially surprising as the deep molding of the leg is carried up onto the dies above.

There are several pieces in the Hennage collection with the square-sectioned straight leg that became popular in both Philadelphia and Newport toward the end of the Chippendale period. This card table achieves distinction through its finely gadrooned skirt, delicate C-scroll brackets, and the retention of its original fire-gilt drawer handles. Elegant gold-plated hardware of this kind, fashionable in Philadelphia during the Chippendale period, was imported from England.

This handsome looking glass is another of the boldly architectural glasses that the Hennages have acquired. The steep scroll of its top, with the bold eagle finial, combine to make a powerful statement. In a relatively small room, the receding vistas reflected in the glass lend a sense of space and intrigue appropriate to the rococo aesthetic. The glass was purchased from Bernard Levy, who acquired it from a direct descendant of the Van Rensselaer family. This gentlemen, whose dress

and social graces left something to be desired, had been shown the door by several prominent New York dealers. He was carrying with him an old and faded photograph of the looking glass, but none of the dealers had recognized its importance. Levy did, and was delighted to be able to purchase it. He was perhaps even more delighted to have picked out this important piece when his various competitors had failed to do so. It is such challenges that make the pursuit of antiques fascinating.

The Upper Stairhall

Climbing the stairway to the second floor, one immediately gets the sense that the upper story will have as much to offer as the rooms below. The upper stairhall, as with all spaces in the house, is furnished with handsome antique pieces chosen with care. Even before reaching the second floor, the visitor encounters an imposing clock on the landing. This very distinguished English tall clock of about 1700 was the first antique the Hennages bought. At the time, before Joe Hennage had given much thought to the idea of collecting antiques, he found the dealer's four-figure asking price appalling. "Why," he said to June, "You can buy a new Lincoln Continental for that amount of money."

He probably would have decided against the purchase—and perhaps against collecting at all—if the dealer hadn't had the wit to send the clock down for the Hennages to try out. The truck drove up just as Joe was turning to the phone to call the dealer with a negative decision. As long as it had arrived, he agreed to look at the clock in the house. He and June haven't stopped buying antiques since.

Like the Pennsylvania tall clock in the hall below, this English example represented its original owner's very considerable status. The tall-clock form had been developed in England during the last forty years of the seventeenth century and represented an enormous step forward in accurate timekeeping. Both clock face and case are ornamented with elaborate scrolling, although the former is brass and the latter is wood veneered in a delicate "seaweed" pattern. The London clockmaker Thomas Planner, member of the Clockmakers Company from 1694-1730, signed the clock's dial.

The upper stairhall at Hennage

House, like those of the eighteenth century, is arranged as an informal social space. The sense of light and openness that is characteristic of the house permeates the upper stairhall as well. Flanking the stairwell are two striking pieces that catch the eye, a pair of gaming tables. Gaming became increasingly popular throughout the eighteenth century, and tables such as these were made to accommodate the pastime. This pair also embodies the new style that became fashionable at the end of the eighteenth century—the neoclassical or Federal style, as it is known in America. Their half-round shapes, square-sectioned tapering legs, and light-wood oval inlay are all features of neoclassical design. A virtually identical card table, pictured in Hewitt, Kane, and Ward, is stamped with the initials of its makers, Samuel and William Fiske, who worked in Salem, Massachusetts. It, like these tables, had a drawer concealed in the frame; this unusual feature is characteristic of tables from Massachusetts and New Hampshire.

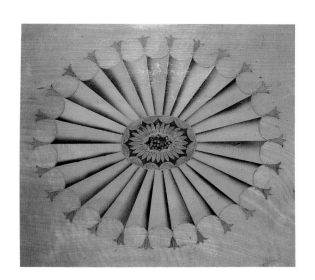

These two appealing English Pembroke tables flank the sofa in the upstairs hall. Both are of satinwood, with crossbanding rimming their tops and central inlaid ovals composed of contrasting dark and light rays. These small tables are the antithesis of the weighty, permanently positioned chest-on-chests at either end of the upper hallway, for they typify the movable furnishings that became especially popular during the neoclassical period.

With their drop leaves and cast-ers, such tables could either be stored against the side of the room or brought out for informal dining and other gatherings. The drawer offers both storage and visual variety to the facade of the piece. Finally, the interesting composition of the intricately detailed inlays is enhanced by the presence of the enamelled silver pulls on the drawer. Such delicate design stood in marked contrast to the heavier concepts that dominated earlier in the century.

When the Hennages finally found the American camelback sofa that now stands downstairs in the parlor, they had come to admire the lines and proportions of this very similar English model so much that they couldn't part with it. It now welcomes guests in the upstairs hall. Not a common form even in the richest colonial cities, the sofa required a cabinetmaker with a sure eye for line and proportion and an owner wealthy enough to purchase the yards and yards of fabric necessary to upholster it.

Two chests stand against the walls, one at either end of the hallway. This imposing Philadelphia chest-on-chest embodies several traditional American collecting ideas. Its impressive size and masterful carving qualify it for inclusion in the category of most wanted American antiques—a classification given cachet a hundred years ago by the dashing gambler/collector Howard Pendleton of Providence, Rhode Island. His antique-filled house conveyed a sense of luxury, of taste, and of a refined American past—and when his interiors were installed in Pendleton House in Providence, they became the first set of exhibition rooms in America to embody those particular ideas.

Many collectors from then until now have shared Pendleton's vision and as a result have collected sophisticated urban furniture. This chest-on-chest, for example, formerly belonged to Mrs. George Maurice Morris, a collector of American antiques whose colonial home, The Lindens, was one of Washington, D. C.'s showplaces. Mrs. Morris had bought the house from Israel Sack, and he consulted on its furnishing. Sack's son Albert, author of one of the first books on connoisseurship in antiques, judged this chest "best" in his well-known "good, better, best" comparisons of American furniture. "The bold carved shell and vines are done by a master carver," he wrote. "This piece has exceptional proportions, not having too wide a body."

In eighteenth-century Philadelphia, chest-on-chests, like high chests, were placed in bedchambers for the storage of clothes. This triangular-pedimented example is less common than the broken-scroll variety, but in both types the use of a pierced rather than a solid scroll board gives the piece a lighter, more graceful appearance. The delicately carved urn-and-flowers finial foreshadows the dainty classical and abstract floral designs of the oncoming neoclassical period.

Rectangularity, symmetry, and classical pediments and pilasters—all derived in the eighteenth century from the classically based architecture of the Palladians—are characteristics also visible in case furniture of that period. Large storage pieces like this lent themselves particularly well to architectural proportions and trim. In combination with the strongly figured mahogany of the drawer fronts, these features made a bold statement of the importance of the piece. Not incidentally, the form is saved from becoming heavy and overbearing by its few nonarchitectural features—the latticework, central finial, and ogee bracket feet. The various elements combine into a masterful result that is large without appearing massive, that is spare yet elegant.

The Private Rooms

Coral is one of June's favorite colors, and she has used various tones of it in the master bedroom for walls, carpet, and upholstery. Nearly all the antique furniture in the master bedroom is from New England—unusual in this house. The mantelpiece in this room is much simpler than the one in the library directly below, but the two are similar in basic architectural treatment. On the mantel, again, are Chinese objects, two of porcelain and one of lacquer. Above the mantel hangs an impressionistic city scene by Edouard Cortes, a French artist who painted many evocative Paris scenes in the early years of this century. Joe loves this painting, which he says gives him great pleasure as he sits beside the fire in the late afternoon and early evening. The colors of the painting, of the flames from the fire, and of the setting sun merge to give a radiant glow to the end of the day.

This English giltwood looking glass demonstrates a complete departure from the architectural forms that dominated American preferences in the late eighteenth century. Gone are the pediments and scrolls

the classical allusions to the past. This is a pure statement of the rococo taste, an intentional rejection of that earlier aesthetic. Light and open, asymmetrical and naturalistic, it is perhaps best described as playful.

Daniel King, Philadelphia's best brass founder during the pre-Revolutionary era, made and signed a pair of andirons now at Winterthur that are very like these, the principal difference being in the shape of the finials. King also sent John Cadwalader, one of Philadelphia's richest and most fashionable citizens, a bill for andirons in 1770: "one Pare of the Best Rote [wrought] fier Dogs With Corinthen Coloms, £25." Unfortunately, the present whereabouts of Cadwalader's andirons is unknown, so we don't know exactly how they looked.

With clean outlines enhanced only by simple fluting and gadrooning, these andirons reflect the linear neoclassical style that Robert Adam introduced to England's aristocracy upon his return from Italy in the late 1750s. Remnants of the previous naturalistic style remain in bold details such as the claw-and-ball feet, but the new style is clearly in the ascendant.

A common furniture form found in bedchambers of the period is the chest of drawers. This chest, of a lovely honey colored mahogany, is very like the one in the library, except that this one has straight bracket feet while the other example has claw-and-ball feet. Blocked furniture appeals to June and Joe, who have a small group in this style from Boston and Newport. John Taylor (1743-1825), a merchant of Salem, Massachusetts, whose ships sailed from home port to Baltimore, New Orleans, and London, was the original owner. The chest descended in Taylor's family.

Another form typically found in eighteenth-century bedchambers is the easy chair. Such chairs provided a comfortable place to sit, especially for the aged or infirm, who may have used them for sleeping as well. The claw-and-ball easy chair in the library shares many features with this Rhode Island pad-footed example in the master bedroom. Its simple, curving lines flow from one section into the next, forming a graceful outline unbroken by any sort of ornament. June chose a pink-coral damask for its covering while Joe worked with the upholsterer to assure a job in which his "tight" approach was followed. The result clearly justified the effort.

In commenting on this chair, Harold Sack wrote that it "has the unusual feature of having a balloon-type seat frame with bowed front and shaped stiles, rather than the conventional straight sides. . . . Expertly reupholstered, this chair stands among the top rated examples for form, quality, and condition."

Reverse serpentine or "oxbow" chests are less common than their serpentine kin. Because of Massachusetts's strong preference for shaped case pieces, this chest of drawers was formerly considered a product of that region. A recent reexamination of the chest's interior and construction suggests that a reconsideration of that conclusion may be in order. One alternative possibility, based on construction techniques and secondary woods, is Charleston, South Carolina.

Another chest of drawers in the collection, like many other pieces made in eastern Connecticut, incorporates features from furniture centers both near and far—here there are suggestions of Rhode Island, Massachusetts, New York, and Pennsylvania practices. The top and base with heavy stepped moldings, distinctive ogee bracket feet with sharp front corners, and stop-fluted columns all show Rhode Island influence, while the practice of inseting quarter columns on the front corners of the case is a Pennsylvania feature. The serpentine facade is reminiscent of the shaped case pieces of Massachusetts, but its deep, bold sweep suggests the vigorous curves of the finest New York gaming tables. Although the strong serpentine line and assertive base molding accent the horizontal aspects of the case, the inlaid rectangles paired on each drawer front and the alternating columns of concave and convex movement create balancing verticals.

The chest is made of cherry, Connecticut's most popular furniture wood, and retains its original silvered brasses—a very unusual feature and one the Hennages prize greatly.

Nearly one whole wall of the master bedroom displays the Hennages' remarkable assemblage of miniature furniture. Little has been written about this engaging subgroup, and even interested scholars and collectors have not come close to answering all the questions that arise as they study these small objects. But collectors through the ages have been fascinated by miniatures: many of them are as carefully constructed as their larger counterparts, their creators having worked with special care to make lilliputian dovetails and to add tiny pieces of veneer and inlay.

Students currently believe that miniatures were made for one of three purposes: to serve as furniture makers' samples, as dollhouse furnishings, and as children's toys. Some pieces seem large enough to have been children's furniture, which makes a fourth category. If these suppositions are correct, the best made and most highly ornamented examples would have been used by cabinetmakers to show off their skills to prospective customers. Less carefully crafted specimens could have been used in dollhouses or in children's rooms.

Beside the miniature display stands the "grandmother" clock, and on the adjacent walls are a landscape by Jasper Cropsey and three cheerful summer views by E. L. Henry. Henry, the well-known colonial-revival painter, is famous for his rural scenes, evocations of a bygone era and carefree days in the country.

Although appearing with the miniatures, this clock functioned just like any other type of timekeeping device. The "grandmother" clock is a rarer form than its counterpart, the "grandfather" clock; it is similar in

design but not as tall as the "grandfather." On this finely made case, beautifully cast brass urn-shape finials stand on plinths that are stop-fluted with brass. Free-standing columns on the case front are likewise stop-fluted and trimmed top and bottom with brass. The clock's painted dial, signed by Allen Kelley of Sandwich, Massachusetts, sports a sweep second hand and striking and alarm mechanisms—a clock collector's dream.

Joe Hennage says that when he bought this clock it was the only time he ever beat Harold Sack out of an antique. Joe had seen the clock earlier at Kindig's shop in Pennsylvania and wanted to buy it, but another customer had first refusal. He told Kindig that if the clock didn't sell, he would like very much to have it.

The Baltimore antiques show was being set up a couple of months later and Joe, as a trustee of the show, was

looking over the displays during a pre-show stroll. To his surprise, he found the clock on exhibit in Joe Kindig's booth. He paused to admire it once again, and just then Harold Sack came by. Joe says that Harold "went bananas" and started talking about buying the clock. Joe didn't say anything. He simply walked down to the front door and stood there until Joe Kindig came in. He hadn't gotten a word out before Kindig, knowing exactly why he was there, said, "It's yours." They shook hands and Joe Hennage went happily back upstairs only to have a very unhappy Harold Sack confront him. It took a visit to Kindig's booth to confirm Joe's story—but Harold finally acknowledged Joe's prior claim. Having revived, and recovered his fighting spirit, Harold offered to buy the clock from Joe Hennage, as it seemed impossible to buy it from Joe Kindig. But it wasn't for sale, and it has become one of the Hennages' treasured pieces.

The miniatures represent all forms of furniture and include all the details of their full-sized brethren. This captivating slant-front desk opens to reveal cubbyholes, drawers, and a central door just as its larger counterparts do. On the exterior, the walnut veneer is crossbanded with herringbone borders while quarter columns ornament the corners of the case. The scale of all the elements of this desk is perfect for its size, adding to its importance among miniatures.

"One of the finest and rarest of all miniatures," says Harold Sack of this canopied bed, and Joe Kindig III, from whom the Hennages bought it, confirms that judgment. This bed is from Pennsylvania, and its foot posts with turned columns and Marlborough legs are a characteristic Philadelphia feature. No high post bed would be complete without bed curtains, of course, and June gave considerable thought to this problem. Her good friend Irma Miller offered to make them. Irma was not only a collector and accomplished needlewoman, but had long been actively involved with the preservation of Chestertown, Maryland. Her hangings complete the effect of this handsome miniature.

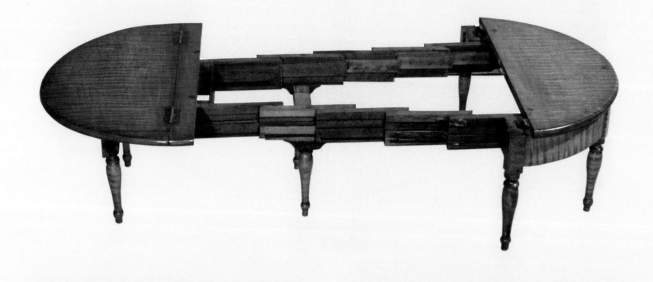

No furniture form seemed too complicated to produce in miniature. This Sheraton curly maple dining table has three removable leaves that allow the table to adjust to several sizes. It was made around the first years of the nineteenth century, probably in New York or New Jersey. When closed, the table presents a unique half-round console design.

Like the dining table, this charming miniature four-poster with serpentine canopy is made of curly maple, but it probably hails from Pennsylvania. Hornor points out that curly maple was much admired in the eighteenth century and was employed for some of the most fashionable Philadelphia forms during the Queen Anne and Chippendale periods. Its decorative wavy grain shows up admirably in the posts and headboard.

We often associate highly figured maple with American, and particularly New England, furniture. In fact, figured maple was harvested and greatly prized in Europe and England at least as early as the seventeenth century. Its use in America was a natural extension of that earlier popularity. The exact reason for the figuring is not known, but it does not occur in all maples. Thus, in 1739 the Boston *Gazette* carried an advertisement, "Whoever has got any curious Maple Tree knots to sell may hear of a Purchaser from the Publisher."

This appealing miniature tea table is, says Harold Sack, "generally acknowledged to be one of the rarest of American furniture" forms. Its straight tapering cabriole legs and turned pad feet are simpler renderings of high-style elements, and its bold porringer ends are also a stylish feature. The table descended in the Brown-Ives family of Newport, Rhode Island, where it is believed to have been made.

This New England child's comb-back Windsor chair is a rare form that has graced two previous collections. The first was that of Mrs. J. Amory Haskell, the New Jersey collector whose house is reputed to have been so full of antiques that one walked from room to room through aisles stacked high on either side. The second was that of Mitchel Taradash, a discriminating Westchester County, New York, collector who lived more conventionally among antiques of the highest quality, storing the overflow in a warehouse.

The Hennage collection boasts a range of forms. Block and serpentine fronts can be seen in the same room with bombé cases, all suggesting the wide scope of the cabinetmaker's imagination. This variety is evident in the miniature collection as well. This handsome mahogany chest of drawers, with a serpentine front and top setting off its graduated drawers, bears testimony to the skill of its Massachusetts maker. That this must have been a special piece is evident from the ogee bracket feet, the string inlay down each corner, and the carefully placed silver escutcheons.

According to Harold Sack, a miniature chest of drawers combining branch birch or satinwood with mahogany veneers rarely comes to light. Full-size chests in this style are attributed to northeastern Massachusetts and southern New Hampshire, so it is likely that a cabinetmaker in that region made this to show off his not inconsiderable skills to prospective customers.

"The scale of the detailing of this piece makes it a gem among surviving miniatures and ranks it as the finest of the three known blockfront miniature chests," wrote Joe Kindig III when the Hennages purchased the chest. It is from Boston, where the blockfront style was fashionable throughout the Queen Anne and Chippendale periods, and it complements nicely the larger Massachusetts blockfront pieces in the Hennage collection. A charming extra is the contemporary hand-blocked wallpaper that lines the chest's drawers.

With its splayed feet and elaborate inlay, this miniature chest belies its size at first glance. The owner's initials are joined by highly elaborated geometric string inlay, probably of holly; such work was characteristic of rural Pennsylvania, especially Chester County. At its best, as in this piece, it lends a charming element of naiveté to what would otherwise be a very formal piece.

This blanket chest is similarly equipped with all the features of its larger counterparts. It is made of walnut that retains its fine old patina, furnished with fashionable brass hardware, including carrying handles, and has a covered till inside. Given the level of construction and finish, it seems likely to have been a cabinetmaker's sample, though it would certainly offer enviable housing to any well appointed doll's wardrobe.

Like the *RF* chest, this chest of drawers was made in Chester County, Pennsylvania. Built of cherry, it has the inset quarter columns that are characteristic of that area. The arrangement of the drawers of this miniature chest of drawers echoes the designs of its larger brethren. The details of the columns and the bracket feet look so much like those of larger examples that if one saw only this picture without knowing its size it could easily be mistaken for a full-sized chest.

A Ballade of Penny Toys

Behold, upon the carpet spread
The nursery cupboard's disarray;
Blue, brown, and orange, green, and
    red,
The friendly toys of every day.
From the tangled heaps of colours
    gay,
From whistles, trumpets, drums and
    noise,
I made this book. Once glance, I
    pray!
This is the Book of Penny Toys.

So Mabel Dearmer began the poem that introduced her *Book of Penny Toys* in 1899, in the midst of the period of greatest popularity for these diminutive playthings. Made in vast numbers in Nuremberg, Germany, and exported to England, France, and the United States, penny toys took their name from their price. They were sold for a penny each in shops and by street vendors, mainly in the years between 1895 and 1914.

Though they could be made of a number of materials, including paper, plaster, wood, and die-cut lead alloy, the most attractive and widely collected examples were made of lithographed tin. In this process very thin sheets of tin were stamped with many tiny fully colored images of objects. Each pre-stamped image was then cut out of the large sheet and bent into its intended shape; it's a little like cutting out paper dolls and their clothes. All kinds of worldly commodities and activities were pressed into penny toy service, and they thus reflected the pre-World War I era in which they were made. Locomotives, fire engines, ambulances, military vehicles, automobiles, airplanes, merry-go-rounds, men sawing a log, dirigibles, mice, and baby buggies were among the diverse subjects available for a penny. Penny toys were among the smallest of popular playthings. They never measured more than ten inches overall and many were much smaller.

June and Joe began collecting these brightly colored trinkets years ago with the idea of trimming the Christmas tree with them. As they added more examples, toys that wouldn't fit on the tree filled the space under and around it. The collection now numbers in the hundreds, and it has become important in its own right, beyond its seasonal role.

The toys in the collection include many of the classics of the penny toy form. The balloon, for instance, is complete with an aerialist whose arms move and an announced destination, Mars. It was made by the firm of Ernest Paul Lehmann, of Brandenburg. Many of the other toys shown here were products of the well-known firm of J. Ph. Meier, of Nuremburg. The embossed dog cart trademark used by that firm became synonymous with the smaller action toys of the period. Among the particular rarities of these small toys are the lady riding sidesaddle and the mother pushing a baby carriage.

Transportation toys came in all shapes and sizes, though they were typically larger in scale than the small action toys. In one way or another, all modes of transport were fair game, whether in the air, on the water, or on the land. The Hennages have a wide range of trains and early automobiles, as well as representatives of the other types. Some are mute as to their origins. Others, like the Lehmann's Autobus produced by the Lehmann firm of Brandenburg, proclaim their manufacturing origins proudly. Each toy, whether performing musician or wheeled rolling stock, bears proudly the scars and wear marks that are the badge of a truly successful toy.

A Home for the Collection

"It's as if you had to be Sherlock Holmes to build this house," said Joe a couple of years after Hennage House was finished. If you can finally build your dream house and you want everything to be exactly right, he was saying, you have to do a lot of sleuthing to find all the components. Bricks—where do you find them with that lovely old-rose glow? Glass—it has to keep out noise and air and ultraviolet rays—does anybody make glass like that? Heat and air conditioning—how do you install a super system that doesn't

show *at all?* Each of these and dozens of other vital ingredients required endless hours of research, making preparation time far greater than actual building time.

Joe and June had taken the first step toward acquiring their own Williamsburg home some years earlier. Joe had heard that Colonial Williamsburg was having trouble raising the money to restore some of the eighteenth-century houses in the Historic Area. He told President Carl Humelsine that he and June would be glad to pay for the renovation of an old house in return for a life-tenancy arrangement—that is, a guarantee that the house would be theirs for the rest of their lives and would not revert to the Foundation until after both their deaths. Humelsine agreed, and Joe remembers

An architect's rendering of a restored Providence Hall, prepared under the Hennages' direction.

Providence Hall.

that "we spent a year looking at and reviewing several opportunities, until Carl called and said he had the perfect house for us to restore." Colonial Williamsburg had recently signed a long-term lease with a local foundation for the use of some land adjacent to the Williamsburg Inn. The property included an eighteenth-century Virginia house known as Providence Hall. It had been moved from the path of a superhighway and thus preserved, but it needed extensive repairs and modernization to be habitable. Despite its dilapidated condition, the house appealed to Joe and June and they were soon at work with an architect and a contractor, developing plans and acquiring materials.

As Joe tells the story, the day before they were to sign the contract that would finalize the arrangement and allow them to begin the actual restoration process, he received an urgent phone call from Carl Humelsine. Humelsine informed him that there was a legal problem and asked that he and June come down to Williamsburg for a meeting that very night. Over dinner, Humelsine told them that complications had developed with regard to the long-term lease and said there might be a delay in straightening it out. June and Joe were flabbergasted. They replied that they needed to think about the situation and spent most of that night coming to grips with what this meant for them personally. If a long-drawn-out legal battle took place, it might be years before they could get started on the Providence Hall renovation, and they simply didn't want to endure such a delay. By morning they had decided: they would turn all the plans over to Colonial Williamsburg and bow out of the project.

The next day they were out looking at property in Williamsburg. The following day they went to a party at the home of their friends Bob and Sarah Armistead; having heard of their dilemma, Judge Armistead suggested they look at two modest houses that had just been put up for sale on property adjacent to the Historic Area. Joe and June liked the location, so within a twenty-four hour period they cleared the transaction with the Foundation and bought the two houses. Those two lots, along with an adjoining third lot that already belonged to Colonial Williamsburg, are now the site of Hennage House.

The third lot was the site of a little house the Hennages were already renting from the Foundation while they worked on the project to restore Providence Hall. Nicknamed the Cottage Small, it remained their Williamsburg home for four years. During that time they researched American Georgian houses up and

South England Street before Hennage House was built.

The Cottage Small.

Christmas at the Cottage Small.

June and Joe review Alan Miller's chimneypiece plans at Mount Pleasant.

down the East Coast, worked on plans, built a detailed model of the house they wanted, investigated suppliers, and only then began construction.

In order to determine just what they did and didn't want in their house, Joe and June traveled widely. "We went to every Georgian house in Maryland, Virginia, Pennsylvania, up into Massachusetts, and down into the Carolinas to look at what the masters did," says Joe. Finally they settled on two of Philadelphia's finest Georgian houses, Mt. Pleasant and the Powel House, as their primary models. With Richard Newlon, their architect, and sometimes also with Alan Miller, their furniture restorer, they measured and photographed. Joe also pored over articles in *The White Pine Series of Architectural Monographs* for architectural ideas.

Finally, Joe made a set of rough sketches of what he and June agreed they wanted: a graceful house in the Georgian style, with a symmetrical facade and a center hall. They wanted a formal parlor and dining room, a library that could also serve as an informal sitting room, and a kitchen that would be practical for both simple meals and large elegant parties. They added

Architect Floyd Johnson with the model of Hennage House.

Scale model of house interior with custom furniture used to design the rooms.

guest suites downstairs in the main part of the house and in the two flanking dependencies, and situated the master bedroom suite upstairs at the back of the house. The "boardroom" is another suite on the basement level that can be used for meetings or parties. The staff of Newlon's office used Joe's sketches as a guide in producing a model of the house.

While the model was in progress, the Hennages found two or three companies that made dollhouse furniture. They bought tiny replicas of each piece in their furniture collection—about two hundred objects—so that they could furnish the model and see how their collection and the spaces worked together. When they learned that there were no ready-made dollhouse-size upholstered pieces, they found someone to create custom replicas of their easy chairs and sofas.

The finished model, made of cardboard on a scale of one inch to the foot, enabled them to rearrange the rooms until they were satisfied that the furnishings worked just the way they wanted them to within each room. At the same time, they were developing the whole design, studying architectural details, and considering exactly what arrangements would suit them best in everyday living. Although they examined many colonial Georgian buildings and adapted features for their own use, Joe feels strongly that their house isn't a copy but is a unique dwelling. Of it, he says proudly, "June and I are responsible for the concept, layout, and design of Hennage House."

When they were satisfied that the model reflected the house they wanted, June and Joe asked the architect to draw up a set of plans. They weren't entirely happy with these, so they went for help to Ed Kendrew, who had guided Colonial Williamsburg's architectural program for many years. Kendrew suggested they show the plans to Floyd Johnson, formerly of Co-

Scale model of house interior.

lonial Williamsburg but by that time head of his own firm and engaged in renovations at Monticello, Thomas Jefferson's home. After a persuasive phone call from Kendrew, Johnson agreed to help the Hennages, though he stipulated that he only had time to consult on the design and could not handle the actual working drawings. The resulting final plans were thus a cooperative effort on the part of two architects and the Hennages.

While work on the model and the plans was going forward, Joe began looking into sources for the various materials needed for the building stage. Because the Hennages think of this as their ultimate house—the one that meets all their requirements and fulfills all their dreams—each part of it had to be carefully thought out and planned for. Nothing was left to chance, and, as Joe has said, you could never "go to any one person and say, 'We want this as a package,'" because each thing had to be separately researched and, often, custom made.

Joe has a history of seeking out innovative building materials. Some years ago, when he moved his business to an irreparably pitted and dirty brick building in downtown Washington, he needed to find a way to conceal the facade without cutting off light and air. He worked with a manufacturer to create a textured metal covering that succeeded both aesthetically and practically, with the result that he met his own needs precisely *and* got credit for encouraging the development of a new product. Another time he worked with a ceiling company to develop a soundproof substance that cut the noise in his pressroom by more than one-half. So it's not surprising to learn that he worked with suppliers of all sorts to get materials and products for his house that did exactly what he and June wanted them to.

The decorative scrolls on the staircase, for example, represent Joe's zest for searching out and using interesting details. He found the pattern in that wonderful architectural treasure trove, *The White Pine Series of Architectural Monographs,* which recorded and described early American buildings and details. First he xeroxed the scroll and then he had the xeroxed image blown up to the size he and June decided was appropriate so that the carpenters could use it as a pattern. Then when the stairs were being installed, Joe revived what he says is the old custom of including concealed coins in a new building. George Washington's and Thomas Jefferson's portraits appear on the quarter and nickel that lie beneath the two newel posts of the main staircase, while Ben Franklin's likeness decorates the silver dollar and two postage stamps beneath one of the posts of the stairway to the downstairs boardroom. It tickles Joe to surmise that "200 years from now people will wonder what we meant by doing that."

In planning their heating system June and Joe wanted to avoid radiators and grills, but when Joe suggested an alternative solution he was told it wouldn't work. Refusing to give up, he worked out a method for

Staircase scrolls adapted from The White Pine Series.

Hennage Creative Printers with bronze anodized aluminum exterior finish.

Putting coins under the newel post.

Nailing down the heart pine floors.

Joe sorting bricks for Hennage House.

June comparing modern bricks to their period counterparts, in search of a perfect match.

returning air through nearly invisible holes in the dentil molding, and the heating contractors were forced to concede that his system worked. From the very convincing imitation logs and automatic pilots in all the fireplaces to the elegant brass bathroom fixtures, everything represents research and extra effort. The cleverly concealed tent-pole holes on the terrace, which Joe devised, and the temperature-controlled wine closet are other examples of purposeful planning.

Joe and June wanted old wood for the floors, and they finally found it close by—two-hundred-year-old heart pine beams that had been taken from a cotton mill in Louisiana built about 1850 and were being stored in Richmond. Their supplier, E. T. Moore, agreed to cut the beams into thicknesses and lengths suitable for flooring. He also cut tongue and groove joints so that each board would fit snugly into the next, and when the floor was installed everything matched up perfectly.

Finding an ironmonger who could design and make the front gates and the balcony over the front door was another challenge. Joe first tried the master blacksmith at Colonial Williamsburg, but he said it would be four or five years before he could do such a job. Craftsmen in the District of Columbia, Pennsylvania, and New Mexico gave similarly bleak estimates, but finally someone suggested Krug and Company, founded in Baltimore in 1805. Not only could they do the job within the required time period, but they were also willing to spend hours with the Hennages getting the designs just right. Recalling the project, Joe says, "You don't know how difficult it is to get a design that doesn't look oddball." They didn't want to copy anything exactly, but they did want their ironwork to be in the Georgian spirit. When Joe announced that he wanted a pineapple, symbol of hospitality, as the central ornament in the balcony design, Krug said "Certainly" and sent him out to buy a fresh pineapple for size. Joe's final contribution to the project was selecting a superior specimen and holding it in the center of the ironwork balcony to see whether it gave the desired effect. The consensus was that it looked fine so Krug first made a wax model, then a wooden one, and then a bronze casting which, when gilded, produced the welcoming pineapple now visible on the Hennage House balcony.

Bricks, too, required research, and the Hennages visited five brickyards to find the two they chose—one to supply bricks for the walls, the other to supply bricks for use around windows, doors, and other open-

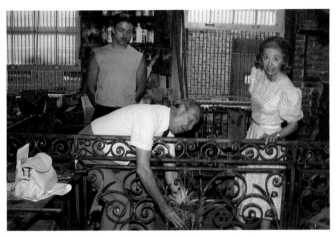

Joe tries out a pineapple in the balcony railing.

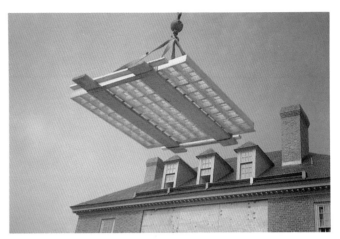

The glass blocks going into position in the porch roof.

A sample wall was built to ensure that all the elements integrated properly.

The glass blocks let in plenty of light.

ings. Because he is always curious about how things work, Joe was fascinated by the brickmaking process, which still relies on hand labor. Once the bricks were on the house site, Joe pitched in to sort them so that the detail bricks would match each other as well as the wall bricks—a time-consuming task.

The glass blocks that form the terrace roof also required a good deal of investigation. Putting a roof over the part of the terrace closest to the house would give June a private sunbathing space just off the master bedroom. Using glass blocks, however, would ensure that the library, the room directly below the bedroom, still got plenty of light. The Hennages knew that glass blocks were in use in New York City at Lincoln Center and at one or two restaurants, so they went up to look at them and to talk to people at those establishments before getting in touch with the manufacturer. Even buying window glass was time consuming because of all the specifications it had to meet. Each window contains three panes of glass that deflect noise, provide 80 percent protection against ultraviolet rays (which fade and weaken fabrics and cause

other harmful effects in antique materials), and prevent outside temperatures from interfering with the interior temperature-control system. It took many hours of conferring with different glass companies to work out the formula the Hennages used.

Both June and Joe wanted a very special parlor fireplace, as that was a major feature of grand eighteenth-century Georgian houses. "With us no article in a well-finished room is so essential," wrote Isaac Ware, speaking of the fireplace in English houses in his *Complete Body of Architecture* of 1756. "The eye is immediately cast upon it on entering, and the place of sitting down is naturally near it. By this means, it becomes the most eminent thing in the finishing of an apartment. . . ." The days when one could find beautiful *old* mantelpieces are long gone, however, and although the Hennages did find an old fireplace wall for the dining room, there wasn't one on the market that was elegant enough for the parlor. Alan Miller, the restorer from Quakertown, Pennsylvania, who has been working with the Hennages on their furniture, is noted for his understanding of high-style

Alan Miller used antique tools to carve the handmade chimneypiece for the parlor.

The chimneypiece goes into place in the parlor.

eighteenth-century Philadelphia carving. Together, he and the Hennages looked at eighteenth-century Philadelphia houses and chose to model their chimneypiece on the very elegant ones at Philadelphia's Cliveden and Powel House. Over a period of more than a year, Miller carved the Hennages' parlor chimneypiece with eighteenth-century tools. When he finally finished, he delivered his work to Williamsburg for installation. Once on the scene, however, he found he couldn't just leave it for someone else, no matter how competent, to install, so he remained to do the job himself. The hearth is made of King of Prussia marble, quarried in the Pennsylvania town of that name and also used in Independence Hall. When Joe and June found this piece of the highly prized stone, they bought it and stored it until they needed it. Their policy of buying especially fine and hard-to-get materials when they found them and storing them for later use began when they were planning the Providence Hall restoration. When that project fell through, they held onto

their stockpiled supplies, eventually using them for the South England Street house.

The fireplace wall in the dining room *is* an old one of about 1760, which S. Dean and Bernard Levy had in storage. Taken from a house in New Castle, Delaware, in 1929, it had been stored since then. When June and Joe heard about it, they went to the Levys' warehouse to look at it and liked it so much they bought it then and there. Thirteen layers of paint had to be removed before they reached the bare wood. Now it is painted a soft putty color that complements the dining room's Chinese porcelains and carpet. The marble hearth here was rescued from an Atlanta, Georgia, house of the mid-nineteenth century. The Hennages found it at a Baltimore company that sells old marble salvaged from houses that are being renovated or torn down.

Before they could begin building, the Hennages had to remove the three houses that occupied their land. Because they have both worked hard all their lives—

June looking at the colonial fireplace wall in a New York warehouse.

Greenspring Manor, the long-since demolished house in New Castle, Delaware, that yielded the dining room fireplace wall.

Joe inspecting chimneys.

June checked often on the progress of construction, always in her pink hard hat.

even as a boy, Joe delivered three different newspapers every day—June and Joe have remained thrifty and practical. So their solution, arrived at in consultation with Colonial Williamsburg, which owned the Cottage Small, was not to destroy but to move the houses and to present them to the city of Williamsburg for use as low-income housing.

The south dependency, the wing to the right of the main house, went up first so that June and Joe could move out of the Cottage Small—the last of the three houses to leave the site—and occupy temporary quarters there. It took three years to finish the house, and the Hennages lived in the south dependency for two of them.

Joe has been closely involved with every aspect of the construction of Hennage House, just as June has thought out and researched every facet of the interior decoration. This house is *theirs* in a very important way, for they carefully considered each step and hand picked each separate element.

Joe's collection of snapshots and slides showing each stage of the building process testifies that he was on hand during construction as much as he could possibly be. If a problem arose, Joe worked on it until an acceptable solution emerged. He talked to the workmen, checked into things, and was very much a part of the project. When all the chimneys were built, for example, Joe climbed ladders up forty-five feet to a platform. While workmen lit a fire in each fireplace, he hovered above, checking to see that each chimney worked properly. The building inspector, standing below on terra firma, said he was pleased to take Joe's word for their functionalism.

As the house took shape, workmen began to prepare the foundations of the brick wall that surrounds the property. In the back, where the Hennage grounds meet the golf course, the bricks rise to a height of eighteen feet—a measure taken to level the ground in the yard and to give the golf course twenty additional feet. Joe had noted while playing golf that the ball

June picking out box bushes at the nursery.

June selecting dogwoods to be moved.

The Raleigh Tavern Society tours Hennage House, 1989.

always seemed to land in those twenty feet and not on the course, so he and June deeded that plot to Colonial Williamsburg. Inside the wall are a variety of trees and shrubs the Hennages chose in consultation with a landscape architect who specializes in Georgian-style gardens. June and Joe went to several nurseries to pick out magnolias, English box, holly, and pink dogwood trees. Although there is a theory that if you surround the roots of a big tree you're planning to move with dirt from its new site, the tree won't know it's been moved, Joe disagrees emphatically. "I can assure you," he says of some of the sizable specimens they brought to Hennage House, "that trees this big *know* when they've been moved." Some didn't survive and others are slowly recovering. When these plants are far enough along, June will begin putting in the gardens and flowers that are her special pleasure.

Finally, Hennage House was built. On Valentine's Day, 1988, the Hennages moved their collection of American antiques to Williamsburg. When June was working out how to run the house, her neighbor Mary Gonzales came forth with what June describes as "one of the nicest gifts I ever received in my life." Mary's

gift was her suggestion that June call Evelyn Funn to see if she could come to help at Hennage House. Happily, Evelyn could come. She helped June put things away after the move and get the main rooms arranged, then began putting the house into the sparkling condition that characterizes it—and that is one of the first things a visitor notices. The spacious rooms, the lovely antique furnishings, and the restful color schemes reflect June's and Joe's thought and taste, but the serene atmosphere that result from orderly and consistent caretaking owes much to Evelyn.

In the fall of 1989, the Hennages entertained the Raleigh Tavern Society, the upper echelon of Colonial Williamsburg's donors, on a warm, sunny afternoon. Guests admired the house and furnishings upstairs and down, peeked into the kitchen, and enjoyed a beautiful tea on the terrace, fitted with an awning for the occasion. The doors were open and a mellow breeze drifted in the front door and out the back. As the last guests were leaving, June said, "I like the house best when we have both doors open and what comes in comes in and we worry about it later." The house shone that day. But even better, so did June and Joe.

Afterword

We have derived great joy and pleasure from the experience of building our collection, and we are delighted to have been able to share some of that experience through this book. We have collected on the principle that the beauty and appeal of the object must come first. Next we considered proportion, detail, authenticity, and finally condition and integrity. Each piece has a story, each brings back a flood of memories, yet each was chosen as part of a whole. The building of this collection has been guided by the knowledge that we would live with it, that the pieces had to function not only alone, but in harmony with all the others. That made the design and construction of the house an integral part of the process. The house, the furnishings, and the garden are ultimately elements of the whole.

It seems especially appropriate that we have been able to bring our collection to Williamsburg. Not only have we come to love this place, but we owe a deep debt of gratitude to Colonial Williamsburg; it has given us much over the years, both in pleasure and in learning. We have been inspired by our experiences here, and they have often informed our decisions. Perhaps most influential of all these experiences has been the Williamsburg Antiques Forum. As we have attended this gathering over the years, we have enjoyed a rare opportunity to listen to scholars of the decorative arts, to learn from others with similar interests, and to know as friends many of our fellow collectors. We have benefitted greatly from the experience.

As we have benefitted, so we hope to be able to benefit others in return. We have gained much from living with these tangible pieces of our American heritage, and from our association with Colonial Williamsburg, and we want to share that experience with others. It is for that reason that we have made arrangements for the collection to come ultimately to Colonial Williamsburg. It is our sincere hope that others will enjoy this collection as we have, and through it will come to a keener appreciation of the world of our forebears.

Finally, we want to express our thanks to the Colonial Williamsburg Foundation for making this book possible, and to John Sands and Penny Stillinger for their steadfast efforts in bringing it to fruition.

June and Joe Hennage

Appendix

The Entrance Stairhall

Page 26
Pair side chairs, walnut, 1760-90, Philadelphia. Height 39 inches, width 22 1/2 inches, depth 17 1/2 inches. See *American Antiques,* Vol. I, p. 6. Provenance: Israel Sack, New York.

Page 27
Serpentine-front chest of drawers, mahogany (pine and poplar secondary), 1770-90, Philadelphia. Height 33 inches, width 46 inches, depth 23 inches. See Federhen, "The serpentine-front chests of drawers of Jonathan Gostelowe and Thomas Jones," in *The Magazine Antiques,* May 1988, pp. 1174-1183. Provenance: descended in the Stryker and Blackwell families of Germantown, PA; Bernard & Dean Levy, New York.

Page 28
Bureau table, mahogany, 1760-90, Philadelphia. Height 32 3/4 inches, width 37 3/4 inches, depth 21 1/2 inches. Provenance: Israel Sack.

Page 29
Looking glass, walnut with gilding, 1760-80, England or America. Height 60 inches, width 30 1/2 inches. The Taradashes' elegantly furnished home was the subject of a "Living with Antiques" article in *The Magazine Antiques* for Jan. 1953, pp. 44-47. Along with other leading collectors of their generation, the Taradashes lent outstanding pieces to "American Art from American Collections," an exhibition sponsored by the newly formed Friends of the American Wing and held at the Metropolitan Museum in 1963. Provenance: ex coll. Mr. and Mrs. Mitchel Taradash, Ardsley-on-Hudson, NY; Israel Sack.

Page 30
Pair looking glasses, walnut with gilding, 1740-60, New York or England. Height 59 1/2 inches, width 31 1/2 inches. These were on loan to the Museum of Fine Arts, Boston, until 1968. Provenance: descended in the Rutgers (collateral relatives of Henry Rutgers, founder of Rutgers University in New Jersey) and De Peyster families. Family letters indicate that Hendrick Rutgers, who married Catherine de Peyster in New York in 1730, originally owned these glasses; Israel Sack.

Page 31
Tall clock, signed on the dial by Laurence Birnie, mahogany (poplar secondary), 1760-75, Philadelphia. Height 102 inches, width 17 1/2 inches, depth 9 inches. Provenance: descended in the Van Wagenen family of Oxford, NY, to Barbara Parker of Albany, NY; Bernard & Dean Levy.

Page 32
Bombé chest of drawers, mahogany, c. 1770, Boston. Height 31 1/4 inches, width 37 3/4 inches, depth 19 1/2 inches. Provenance: this chest was for many years in the personal collection of Mr. and Mrs. Joe Kindig, Jr., York, PA.

Page 33
Design for a "Sideboard Table" from Thomas Chippendale's 1754 *The Gentleman and Cabinet-maker's Director,* Pl. LVI. I am grateful to Jon Prown for calling this design to my attention.

Slab table, mahogany and marble, c. 1770, possibly Rhode Island. Height 33 1/4 inches, width 54 1/2 inches, depth 25 1/2 inches. See Heckscher, p. 155; Chippendale, Pl. LVI; and Gershenson. See also Swan, "American Slab Tables," in *The Magazine Antiques* Jan. 1953, pp. 40-43. Provenance: ex coll. Mr. and Mrs. Charles H. Gershenson, Detroit, MI; Israel Sack.

Page 34
"Virginia, Marylandia, et Carolina," by John Baptist Homann, hand-colored line engraving, c. 1735, Nuremberg. Height 19 inches, width 22 3/4 inches. Provenance: The Book Press, Ltd., Williamsburg, VA.

"Carte De La Virginie et Du Maryland," by Robert de Vaugondy, line engraving, 1755, Paris. Height 19 inches, width 25 1/4 inches. Published in Vaugondy's *Atlas Universal,* Paris, 1757. This is a French edition of the well-known Fry and Jefferson map of Virginia and Maryland, published in London in 1754 or 1755.

See Cooley Verner, "The Fry and Jefferson Map," *Imago Mundi*. Provenance: E. Forbes Smiley III, New York.

Page 35

[The Campaign of 1781]. From François Soulés, *Histoire des troubles de l'Amérique anglaise*, 4 vols. Paris, 1787. Height 10 1/2 inches, width 36 1/2 inches. Provenance: Shreve, Crump & Low, Boston, MA.

"A Plan of Yorktown and Gloucester in The Province of Virginia, Shewing the Works constructed for the Defence . . . British Army . . . ," printed for William Faden, Geographer to the King, Charing Cross, October 7th, 1785. Height 27 3/4 inches, width 21 inches. Provenance: The Old Print Shop, New York.

The Parlor

Page 39

Five-piece garniture, China trade porcelain, Quianlong period, c. 1760, tobacco-leaf design. Height: 5 1/2 to 6 3/4 inches. Provenance: Fred B. Nadler Antiques, New York.

Bracket or shelf clock, signed on the dial "John Crowley / Philadelphia," mahogany case, 1802-10. Height 21 inches, width 12 inches, depth 7 1/4 inches. A John Crawley worked in Philadelphia on Spruce and South Front Streets from 1803 to 1825. George Horace Lorimer of Philadelphia, for many years editor of *The Saturday Evening Post* and a great collector of American antiques, formerly owned this clock. He loved to go antiquing with his friend Kenneth Roberts, who wrote spoofs for the *Post* on the collecting mania of the 1920s. Provenance: ex coll. George H. Lorimer; Bernard & Dean Levy.

Page 40

Easy chair, walnut (white oak and yellow pine secondary), c. 1760, Philadelphia. Height 44 inches, width 34 inches, depth 23 inches. Provenance: Bernard & Dean Levy.

Page 41

High chest, mahogany and mahogany veneers, 1760-90, Philadelphia. Height 97 3/4 inches, width 45 1/2 inches, depth 23 inches. Provenance: descended from Benjamin Franklin or his daughter Sarah Franklin

Bache to Henrietta Bache Jayne, from whom the firm of Ginsburg & Levy acquired it; Ginsburg & Levy, New York.

Page 42

Tea table with "birdcage" attachment, mahogany, 1760-90, Philadelphia. Height 28 3/4 inches, diameter of top 32 inches. Provenance: descended in the family of William Dunn, who founded Dunnstown, PA, in 1786; acquired privately.

Page 43

Easy chair, mahogany, 1770-80, Philadelphia. Height 47 inches, width 37 1/4 inches, depth 23 1/4 inches. Inscribed "McClenachen" in chalk on rear rail. Illustrated: Kindig, No. 70. Provenance: descended in the McClenachen family of Philadelphia; ex coll. William K. du Pont; G.K.S. Bush, Washington, D.C.

Page 44

Looking glass, labeled by John Elliott, Sr. (1713-91), mahogany with gilding, c. 1760, England or Philadelphia. Height 79 1/2 inches, width 28 3/4 inches. Provenance: Joe Kindig III.

Page 45

Dressing table, mahogany, 1760-90, Philadelphia. Height 28 3/4 inches, width 34 3/4 inches, depth 20 inches. Provenance: ex coll. Reginald Lewis, Easton, MD; Joe Kindig III.

Page 46

Looking glass, mahogany with gilding, c. 1760, England or Philadelphia. Height 77 inches, width 32 inches. Provenance: Joe Kindig III.

Page 47

Dressing table, mahogany (poplar and pine secondary), 1760-90, Philadelphia. Height 30 inches, width 35 1/4 inches, depth 19 inches. Illustrated: *The Magazine Antiques,* May 1939, frontispiece; and May 1961, p. 470. According to Bernard Levy, through whom the Hennages acquired the table, the Varicks "had superlative family furniture from many sources, both through marriage and purchases, from Philadelphia, Boston, and New York." Mr. and Mrs. Andrew Varick Stout increased the family collection substantially through their own collecting activities in the 1920s and 1930s. Provenance: descended in the Varick and Stout families of New York; Bernard & Dean Levy.

Page 48
Desk and bookcase, walnut, 1760-90, Philadelphia. Height 103 inches, width 40 inches, depth 23 1/4 inches. Provenance: David Stockwell, Wilmington, DE.

Page 49
Sofa, mahogany (white oak and pine secondary), 1765-85, Philadelphia. Height 39 1/2 inches, width 88 inches, depth 29 inches. Provenance: ex. coll. Richard du Pont; Bernard & Dean Levy.

Page 50
Armchair, mahogany, 1760-90, Philadelphia. Height 40 1/4 inches, width 24 1/2 inches, depth 19 inches. Illustrated: Sack, *Fine Points of Furniture*, p. 32. Provenance: Joe Kindig III.

Page 51
Tea table with rectangular dished top and notched corners, mahogany, 1755-70, probably Boston. Height 28 1/4 inches, width 29 3/4 inches, depth 18 3/4 inches. Provenance: a paper label on the underside of the top reads, "This table belonged to Susanna Shoemaker (a Great Aunt to Grand Mother Hannah Williams) she died early in the century—it is probably 150 years old (H. W. Roberts 1892). There are 2 high backed walnut chairs with loose hair covered seats to go with it. I prize the set very much." A chalk inscription reads: *S. Williams Parti* [illegible]; Israel Sack.

Page 52
Easy chair, mahogany, 1780-95, Newport. Height 47 1/2 inches, width 34 3/4 inches overall. Illustrated: Biddle, No. 40; Moses, Fig. 1.42; see also Moses's discussion of stop-fluted forms, p. 13. Exhibited: Metropolitan Museum of Art, New York. Provenance: Israel Sack.

Page 53
Tripod tea table, mahogany, 1760-70, Philadelphia. Height 28 1/4 inches, diameter of top 31 1/2 inches. Illustrated: *The Magazine Antiques*, Jan. 1941, p. 20, in an article on the Davis collection. The quotations appear in Hornor, p. 140; see also pp. 139 ff. for more information about Philadelphia tea tables. Provenance: ex colls. Herman Clarke, Boston; Israel Sack, Boston; Charles K. Davis, Fairfield, CT; Israel Sack.

Tea service with teapot, covered sugar bowl, and creamer, by Garret Schank (w. 1785-95), silver, c.

1790, New York.   Monogrammed *GP* in script for Gertrude Polhemus of Staten Island, NY. Provenance: Israel Sack.

Page 54
Bureau table or kneehole desk, mahogany, 1755-65, Newport. Height 34 inches, width 37 1/4 inches, depth 18 1/4 inches. Illustrated: Moses, Fig. 1.15 and p. 8. Provenance: Joe Kindig III.

Page 55
Side chairs, set of six, mahogany, c. 1770, Philadelphia. Height 40 inches, width 23 inches, depth 17 1/4 inches. Provenance: Ginsburg & Levy.

Page 56
Looking glass, walnut veneer with gilding, c. 1765, England or America. Height 60 1/2 inches, width 31 inches. Exhibited at the Brooklyn Museum 1955-67. Quote from Comstock, 1968, p. 10. Provenance: descended in the Frisbee family of New York and northern New Jersey (a number of Frisbees served in the Continental Army during the Revolution); ex coll. George Horace Lorimer; Benjamin Ginsburg, New York.

Page 57
An East Perspective View of the City of Philadelphia, in the Province of Pensylvania, in North America; Taken from the Jersey Shore, engraving with original color, first published in 1778. Height 10 15/16 inches, width 16 7/8 inches. See Déak, *Picturing America*, vol. 1, p. 62. Provenance: W. Graham Arader III, King of Prussia, PA.

Pair andirons, cast brass, 1770-80, America. Height 23 1/4 inches, width 13 inches, depth 18 inches. Provenance: ex. coll. John W. Batdorf, Meadowbrook, PA.

The Dining Room

Page 59
Breakfront, mahogany, 1750-60, England. Height 105 inches, width 76 inches, depth 25 inches. Provenance: Arthur Ackerman & Son, New York.

Page 60
Berry dish with Society of Cincinnati emblem and Fitzhugh border, porcelain, c. 1785, part of a dinner service made in China for George Washington.

Diameter 6 1/4 inches, height 1 inch. Provenance: Elinor Gordon, Villanova, PA.

Dinner plate with Society of Cincinnati emblem and Fitzhugh border, porcelain, c. 1785, made in China for George Washington. Diameter 9 3/4 inches, height 1 inch. Exhibited: China Trade Museum, Milton, Mass. Provenance: ex coll. The Dietrich Brothers Americana Foundation; Elinor Gordon.

Dinner plate with Society of Cincinnati emblem and Fitzhugh border, porcelain, c. 1785, made in China for George Washington. Diameter 9 3/4 inches, height 1 inch. Provenance: ex personal coll. Elinor Gordon.

Page 61
Plate with American eagle, porcelain, c. 1800, part of a service ordered from China by Thomas Jefferson. Diameter 9 11/16 inches. Exhibited: U. S. Department of State. Provenance: Elinor Gordon.

Plate with Lee family arms, porcelain, Young Chen period (1723-35), made in China for the English market. Diameter 9 inches, height 1 1/2 inches. Provenance: Fred B. Nadler.

Plate with central Mt. Vernon motif, porcelain, c. 1805, made in China for the American market. Diameter 7 3/4 inches, height 5/8 inch. Illustrated: Howard and Ayers, *China for the West,* Pl. 505, p. 495. Provenance: Fred B. Nadler.

Pair of water bottles, porcelain, Ch'ien Lung period (1736-95), made in China for DeWitt and Maria Clinton of New York City. Height 10 inches. Provenance: Fred B. Nadler.

Pair of dishes decorated with Malcolm Smith's (of Smithtown, Long Island, NY) monogram, porcelain, 1800-20, made to order in China. An example from this set is illustrated in Palmer, p. 73. Provenance: Fred B. Nadler.

Plate with the arms of John Morgan of Connecticut, porcelain, Ch'ien Lung period (1736-95), made to order in China. Provenance: Fred B. Nadler.

Page 62
Sauce tureen with cover and stand, Fitzhugh pattern, porcelain, c. 1800, made in China for the Western trade. Tureen height 5 3/4 inches, width 8 1/4 inches, depth 5 1/4 inches; stand height 1 inch, width 8 inches, depth 6 inches. Provenance: Fred B. Nadler.

Pair of plates, Fitzhugh pattern, porcelain, Tao-Kuang period (early 19th century), made in China for the Western trade. Provenance: Fred B. Nadler.

Pair of pot-de-cremes with covers, Fitzhugh pattern, porcelain, c. 1800, made in China for the Western trade. Provenance: Fred B. Nadler.

Page 63
Five-piece mantel garniture, China trade porcelain, c. 1770. Height 3 1/2 inches to 4 1/4 inches. Provenance: Elinor Gordon.

Miniature white dogs, China trade porcelain, c. 1780. Height 2 1/2 inches, width 4 inches. Provenance: Fred B. Nadler.

Miniature ducks, painted in famille rose colors, China trade porcelain, c. 1790. Height 2 1/4 inches, width 3 1/4 inches. Provenance: Fred B. Nadler.

Page 64
Tea service, China trade porcelain, Qianlong period, c. 1775. Service consists of teapot and stand, cream jug, spoon tray, tea bottle, saucers, tea bowls, and coffee cups. Provenance: Earle D. Vandekar, New York.

Page 65
Arm chair and side chair from a set, mahogany, c. 1795, New York. Height 36 1/4 inches, width 22 1/2 inches, depth 17 3/4 inches. The Hennage collection contains two sets of these chairs of identical design. Six side and two arm chairs descended in the Riker family, and nine side chairs descended in the Davenport family. Design of back from Thomas Sheraton's *Drawing Book of 1794,* Pl. 36, No. 1. Provenance: Ginsburg & Levy.

Page 66
Two-part dining table, mahogany, c. 1810, Boston. Height 27 3/4 inches, width 59 3/4 inches, length 132 inches. Provenance: Joe Kindig III.

Page 68
Tea set with coffee pot, teapot, waste bowl, creamer, and sugar bowl, by John McMullin (1765-1843),

silver, c. 1795, Philadelphia. Monogrammed <u>SSJ</u>. A service with very similar forms and bright-cut monogram encircled by a laurel wreath by Christian Wiltberger, also of Philadelphia, is in the Museum of Fine Arts, Boston (Buhler, vol. 2, No. 530); another, by Joseph Richardson, is in the Philadelphia Museum. Provenance: Israel Sack.

Page 69
Coffee pot, by Richard Humphreys (w. in Philadelphia 1771-91), silver, c. 1775, Philadelphia. Height 13 1/2 inches. Provenance: made for, and descended in, the Taggart family of Pottstown, PA; Bernard & Dean Levy.

Page 70
Miniature portrait of Paul Revere by W. C. Russell (w. in N.Y.C. 1837), oil on ivory, 1830, Boston. Height 4 1/2 inches, width 3 3/4 inches. Inscribed on back: "Paul Revere about 80 years of age Boston 1830." Provenance: ex coll. Susan Revere Edgerley of Canton, MA, a direct descendant of Paul Revere; Israel Sack.

Page 71
Porringer, by Jesse Churchill (1773-1819), silver, c. 1780, Boston. Length 8 1/8 inches, diameter 5 3/8 inches. Provenance: S. J. Shrubsole, New York.

Porringer, by Jacob Hurd (1702-58), silver, c. 1730-58, Boston. Engraved with the initials *PC* for Prudence Chester (1699-1780), wife of J. Stoddard of Northampton, MA. Recorded: French, *Jacob Hurd and His Sons*, addenda, p. 4, No. 149A. Provenance: S. J. Shrubsole.

Porringer, by Benjamin Burt (1729-1805), silver, c. 1750, Boston. Provenance: Gertrude Weber, Brooklyn, NY.

Porringer, by Paul Revere (1735-1818), silver, c. 1785, Boston. Engraved on handle: *PMM.* Cover by another, unidentified, maker. Exhibited: Museum of Fine Arts, Boston. Provenance: Firestone and Parson, Boston.

Porringer, by Daniel Henchman (1730-75), silver, 1755-65, Boston. Engraved on handle: *I.S. to S.S.* Provenance: Israel Sack.

Page 72
Tea set with coffee pot, two teapots, waste bowl, creamer, and sugar bowl, by Littleton Holland (1770-1847), silver, c. 1800, Baltimore. Coffee pot height 12 inches, width 12 3/4 inches; teapot height 10 1/4 inches, width 10 3/4 inches; waste bowl height 4 inches, diameter 6 1/4 inches; sugar bowl height 9 3/4 inches, width 7 1/4 inches; creamer height 6 inches, width 5 1/2 inches. Provenance: monogrammed *K* for Julia Bedford Krebs, grandmother of Mary L. Van Winkle, in whose family the set descended; Israel Sack.

Page 73
Covered jug, by Thomas H. Warner (1780-1828), silver, c. 1805, Baltimore. Height 10 1/8 inches. Illustrated in Pleasants and Sill, Pl. XL. Provenance: descended in the family of the prominent Baltimore merchant Amos Adams Williams; S. J. Shrubsole.

Salver, by Andrew Ellicott Warner (1786-1870), silver, c. 1815, Baltimore. Diameter 11 inches, height 1 1/8 inches. Two oval salvers by Andrew E. Warner with the same delicate snowflake pattern are illustrated in Pleasants and Sill, Pls. XXXVII and XXXVIII. Provenance: S. J. Shrubsole.

Ladle, by Andrew Osthoff (w. Baltimore c. 1809-14, thereafter in Pittsburgh), silver, 1815-25, Pittsburgh. Length 13 1/8 inches. Engraved with the initials *EM* on the face; with *Thompson. 1851* on the underside. Provenance: Adam A. Weschler & Son, Washington, D.C.

Page 74
Teapot, by William Ball (w. 1759-71), silver, c. 1765, Philadelphia. Height 5 3/4 inches. Exhibited: Philadelphia Museum of Art, 1956; see Philadelphia Museum of Art, *Philadelphia Silver, 1682-1800* (No. 25). Provenance: engraved on the side *GP* and in block letters on the base *G. Peel* for Grace Peel, daughter of Philadelphia merchant Oswald Peel; S. J. Shrubsole.

Tankard, by John David (1736-94), son of Peter David, with whom he worked, silver, c. 1763, Philadelphia. Height 7 7/8 inches. Engraved opposite handle with coat of arms, crest, and the initials *L.L.H.* for the Hollingsworth family. Provenance: S. J. Shrubsole.

Soup ladle, by John David, silver, c. 1763, Philadelphia. Length 12 1/2 inches. Provenance: S. J. Shrubsole.

One of a pair of sauce boats, by John David, silver, 1760-75, Philadelphia. Provenance: Jonathan Trace, Putnam Valley, NY.

Page 75

Cann, by Benjamin Burt (1729-1805), silver, 1750-1800, Boston. Height 6 inches. Provenance: made for Forman and Ann Cummings Chessman and descended in the family; Jonathan Trace.

Tankard, by Nathaniel Mors(e) (1685/8-1748), silver, Boston. Height 8 3/4 inches. Information about Mors(e) can be found in Flynt and Fales, *The Heritage Foundation Collection of Silver,* p. 278. Provenance: Bernard & Dean Levy.

Sugar tongs, by Thomas Arnold (1734-1828), silver, 1770-80, Newport. Length 5 1/4 inches. For information about Arnold see, Flynt and Fales, p. 146; Provenance: Israel Sack.

Pepper box, by John Blowers (1710-48), silver, 1741, Boston. Height 3 1/2 inches. Inscribed, "Given to D. Russell/in Remembrance of her/Nephew Sam:ˡl Eliot/ Who died upon the/Coast of Africa 1ˢt of Jan:ʸ/1741 Ae 24." Exhibited: 1952, Seattle, San Francisco, and Los Angeles museums; 1958, Smith College Museum (in "Early New England Silver," cat. no. 19); 1960, London ("American Silver and Art Treasures at the English Speaking Union); 1972-83, Washington, D.C. (Diplomatic Reception Rooms, State Dept.; No. 3 in *Silver Supplement* to guidebook). References: Buhler and Hood, vol. 1, No. 178 and Buhler, vol. 1, p. 264. Provenance: ex colls. Dwight Blaney, an early and avid Boston collector of American antiques with a special interest in silver; and Mark Bortman, a Bostonian of the generation following Blaney's who was an extremely discerning silver collector; William Core Duffy, New Haven, CT.

Page 76

Four salts, by John Adam, Sr. (1755-98), silver, c. 1780, Alexandria, VA. Diameter 2 5/8 inches. Provenance: S. J. Shrubsole.

Page 77

Tea Caddy, by Joseph Richardson, Jr. (1752-1831), silver, 1785-1800, Philadelphia. Richardson, Jr. was the son of Joseph Richardson and, with his brother Nathaniel, trained with his father. The two brothers were in partnership from c. 1771 to 1791. See Buhler, *American Silver 1655-1825*, p. 611. Provenance: ex coll. Mr. and Mrs. Howard Joynt; Christie's, Jan. 10, 1990.

Tea-caddy spoon, by John David, silver, c. 1780, Philadelphia. The stem is engraved with a script "D." Provenance: S. J. Shrubsole.

Page 78

Epergne, by Thomas Pitts (w. 1767-93), silver, 1768, London. Height 15 inches, width 20 inches (without baskets); baskets 5 1/2 to 6 1/2 inches in diameter. For a summary of Edith Gaines's search for the identity of the true *TP*, see "Powell? Potts? Pitts!" in *The Magazine Antiques,* April 1965, pp. 462-65. Provenance: Shaw & Brown, Washington, D.C.

Page 79

Pair of brackets, gilded pine, c. 1760, England. Height 15 3/4 inches, width 7 1/4 inches, depth 5 1/4 inches. Provenance: Bernard and Dean Levy.

Pair andirons, attributed to Richard Wittingham (w. New York, 1806-18), brass, New York. Height 27 inches, width 12 inches, depth 20 3/4 inches. Provenance: Israel Sack.

Page 80

Sideboard, mahogany, mahogany veneers, light, dark, and stained-wood inlays, 1790-1810, Baltimore. Height 38 3/4 inches, width 78 1/4 inches, depth 26 1/2 inches. See Elder and Stokes, pp. 145-46, Fig. 111, for an almost identical example. Provenance: descended in the Twaddell-Davis family of Philadelphia; Ginsburg & Levy.

Page 81

Mirror, or girandole, gilded wood, brass, and glass, 1810-20, England or Boston. Height 45 inches, width 37 inches. Provenance: Israel Sack.

Page 82

Serpentine-front bureau, mahogany and mahogany veneers, 1780-1800, probably Newport. Height 35 inches, width 39 inches, depth 21 1/2 inches. See Moses, p. 57, Fig. 1.47 for a very similar example labeled by Holmes Weaver. Provenance: Israel Sack.

Page 83
Looking glass, gilded wood and painted and gilded glass panels, c. 1800, probably New York. Height 58 1/2 inches, width 26 inches. Provenance: Joe Kindig III.

The Library

Page 87
Looking glass, labeled by Hosea Dugliss (c. 1795-1867) some years after it was made, walnut with gilding (pine secondary), c. 1790, New York. Height 77 inches, width 31 inches. On reverse is an inscription and date. Illustrated, Comstock, 1962, No. 345; *The Magazine Antiques,* May 1965, p. 592, and May 1981, p. 1183. Provenance: Joe Kindig & Son, York, PA; ex colls. Reginald M. Lewis, Easton, MD, and Henry Ford Museum; Bernard & Dean Levy.

Label of Hosea Dugliss on reverse of looking glass. Dugliss was born in England and was at work in New York by 1818. Comments on this looking glass and information about the Dugliss label appear in "More about looking glasses," the 1965 note in *Antiques.* The label shows in barely discernible letters the name of its printer—Robert Sears, who, according to the *Dictionary of American Biography,* was not active in New York until 1832.

Page 88
Arm chair, mahogany (pine secondary), c. 1770, Philadelphia. Height 38 1/2 inches, width 24 1/4 inches, depth 18 1/2 inches. Similar chairs are illustrated in Hornor, Pl. 260 (opp. p. 174; the attribution to Thomas Affleck is now questioned); Jobe and Kaye, Nos. I-14 and I-15 (pp. 20-21); Kane, Nos. 90-93 (pp. 106-112 and Fig. 2, p. 112 for Pl. X of Chippendale's *Director* (1762 ed.), showing the design from which these splats were taken); and Comstock, No. 248. Provenance: Bernard & Dean Levy.

Page 89
Chest of drawers, mahogany, 1760-80, Boston. Height 33 1/4 inches, width 38 inches, depth 21 3/4 inches. See Jobe and Kaye, pp. 138-50, for illustrations and discussions of blocked chests of drawers from Boston and Portsmouth, NH. Harold Sack notes that "The superb quality and condition of this chest places it in a rare echelon of Massachusetts block front chests. The boldness and vigor of execution suggests one of

Boston's greatest artist craftsmen." Provenance: inherited by Mrs. Bradlee Smith of Brookline, MA, a direct descendant of William Penn; ex coll. Mitchel Taradash, Ardsley-on-Hudson, NY; Israel Sack.

Page 90
Card table, mahogany (birch and white pine secondary), c. 1760-80, Newburyport, MA. Height 28 1/4 inches, width 36 inches, depth 18 inches. This table retains its original drawer and handle. According to Harold Sack, a table closely related to this one is in the collections of the St. Louis Art Museum, sold to them by Israel Sack of Boston, the founding patriarch of the Sack firm. Provenance: descended in the Larkin family of Newburyport; Israel Sack.

Page 91
Pair of andirons, brass, 1770-80, America. Height 19 1/4 inches, width 14 inches, depth 15 1/4 inches. Information on Tench Tilghman (1744-86) is from *Encyclopedia of the American Revolution,* by Mark M. Boatner III, 1966, pp. 1108-09. Provenance: descended in the Tilghman family of Maryland and Pennsylvania; Leon F. S. Stark, Philadelphia.

Page 92
Armchair, walnut, 1760-90, Philadelphia. Height 40 1/2 inches, width 25 1/4 inches, depth 17 1/2 inches. Provenance: ex coll. Albert Whittier, Boston; Israel Sack.

Page 93
Easy chair, mahogany, 1760-70, Boston. Height 45 3/4 inches, width 34 3/4 inches, depth 31 inches. Biographical material on General Danielson is from *Appleton's Cyclopedia of American Biography* and *Massachusetts Soldiers and Sailors of the Revolutionary War* (Boston, 1896). This chair was first illustrated in *The Magazine Antiques* in Dec. 1930, p. 536, in the "Queries and Opinions" column, the family having apparently sent a snapshot for identification; Homer Eaton Keyes, then *Antiques's* editor, pronounced it a "noble old chair" of 1745-55. Several very similar chairs have been published, among them No. 102 (pp. 265-69) in Jobe and Kaye, and No. 68 (p. 77) in Greenlaw; see also Heckscher, 1971, frontispiece and pp. 886-93. Provenance: Timothy Danielson (1733-91), original owner, left the chair to his daughter Sarah, through whom it descended in the Lincoln and Peirce families; Israel Sack.

Page 94
Armchair, mahogany, c. 1770, Philadelphia. Height 42 inches, width 28 inches, depth 24 1/2 inches. Hornor illustrates several variants of the upholstered-back, open-arm Marlborough chair, and discusses them on pp. 224-27. Heckscher, 1985, provides an excellent up-to-date discussion of the form in the caption to illustration No. 69, pp. 117-18. Provenance: Israel Sack.

Page 95
Pair of Pembroke tables, mahogany, 1770-80, Philadelphia. Height 28 1/2 inches, width 38 3/4 inches (extended), depth 29 3/4 inches. Provenance: Israel Sack.

Charleston Bed and Sitting Rooms

Page 97
High chest, cherry, 1740-60, Connecticut. Height 86 inches, width 38 3/4 inches, depth 18 1/2 inches. Illustrated: Wadsworth Atheneum, 1967, No. 84; Cooper, *In Praise of America,* p. 218. Provenance: Israel Sack.

Page 98
Dressing table, mahogany, 1780-1800, Rhode Island. Height 29 inches, width 31 1/4 inches, depth 18 1/4 inches. Quote is from Monkhouse and Michie, p. 88. Provenance: Israel Sack.

Page 99
Bedstead, mahogany and light-wood inlay, c. 1790, Charleston, SC. Height 90 3/4 inches, width 66 inches, depth 78 inches. Provenance: Joe Kindig, Jr.

Page 100
Desk with tambour doors, mahogany and satinwood, 1780-1800, Massachusetts. Height 46 1/2 inches, width 37 inches, depth 30 3/4 inches. See Harold Sack, pp. 119-29, for entertaining personal reminiscences about Clarke and Davis; *The Magazine Antiques,* Jan. and March, 1941, for "Antiques in Domestic Settings," an article on Davis's antiques as they looked in his home; and *American Antiques,* Vol. V. Provenance: ex colls. Herman Clarke, Boston, and C. K. Davis, Fairfield, CT; Israel Sack.

Page 101
Candlestand or tea table with birdcage attachment, mahogany, 1750-70, Philadelphia. Height 27 1/4 inches, diameter of top 21 3/4 inches. Provenance: acquired privately.

Page 102
Sideboard, mahogany and satinwood inlay, c. 1790, northern Massachusetts or New Hampshire. Height 39 3/4 inches, width 22 inches, depth 17 3/4 inches. Illustrated: *American Antiques from the Israel Sack Collection,* Vol. VIII, p. 2373. Provenance: Israel Sack.

Page 103
Two of a set of six side chairs, mahogany, c. 1760-80, Philadelphia. Height 38 1/2 inches, width 22 inches, depth 18 1/4 inches. Provenance: Israel Sack.

Page 104
Chest of drawers, walnut, 1760-70, Philadelphia. Height 33 1/4 inches, width 32 3/4 inches, depth 20 1/2 inches. Provenance: Israel Sack.

Page 105
Drop-leaf table, mahogany (oak secondary), c. 1770, Philadelphia. Height 28 1/2 inches, width 54 inches, depth 44 1/2 inches. Illustrated: Hornor, 1988 ed., p. iv (with caption by Joe Kindig III). Provenance: ex coll. Elvena Price; Bernard & Dean Levy.

Page 106
Card table, mahogany, 1760-80, Philadelphia. Height 30 inches, width 36 inches, depth 17 1/2 inches. Provenance: Israel Sack.

Page 107
Looking glass, mahogany with gilding, 1770-80, England or America. Height 71 1/4 inches, width 28 inches. Provenance: Van Rensselaer family; Bernard & Dean Levy.

The Upper Stairhall

Page 109
Tall clock, signed on the dial by Thomas Planner (free of the Clockmakers Company 1701-30), walnut and light-wood veneer, brass, ormolu, c. 1700, London. Height 96 inches, width 19 1/2 inches, depth 10 inches. Provenance: Arthur S. Vernay, New York.

Pages 110, 111
Pair of gaming tables, mahogany with light-wood inlay, c. 1795, probably Salem, MA. Height 28 inches, width 35 3/4 inches, depth 17 1/2 inches. I wish to thank Jon Prown of Colonial Williamsburg for pointing out an apparently identical table in Hewitt, Kane, and Ward, *The Work of Many Hands: Card Tables in Federal America, 1790-1820,* No. 15. Provenance: R. T. Trump & Co., Philadelphia.

Page 112
Pembroke tables, satinwood with light- and dark-wood inlay, 1780-90, London. Upper: height 28 1/2 inches, width 38 1/2 inches (extended), depth 28 inches. Provenance: Arthur Ackermann & Son. Lower: height 28 3/4 inches, width 38 inches (extended), depth 27 1/2 inches. Provenance: Needham's Antiques, New York.

Page 113
Sofa, mahogany, 1750-65, England. Height 38 inches, width 90 1/2 inches, depth 24 inches. Provenance: Jeannette R. Marks, Lexington, KY.

Page 114
Chest-on-chest, walnut, 1760-90, Philadelphia. Height 99 1/2 inches, width 44 3/4 inches, depth 22 1/2 inches. Illustrated: Albert Sack, p. 118, and Winchester, "Living with Antiques," *The Magazine Antiques* Jan. 1956, pp. 60-63. See also *Antiques* for Feb. 1938 for an earlier article on The Lindens. Provenance: Joe Kindig, Jr.; ex coll. Mrs. George M. Morris; Christie's, January 22, 1983. Provenance: Israel Sack.

Page 115
Chest-on-chest, mahogany, 1770-90, Philadelphia. Height 94 inches, width 44 1/4 inches, depth 22 inches. Provenance: Joe Kindig III.

The Private Rooms

Page 116
Looking glass, glass and gilded wood, c. 1760, England. Height 55 inches, width 28 1/2 inches. Provenance: Benjamin Ginsburg.

Pair of andirons, attributed to Daniel King (w. 1765-95), brass and iron, c. 1795, Philadelphia. Height 23 1/4 inches, width 12 1/2 inches, depth 18 1/2 inches. Provenance: Parke-Bernet Galleries, New York.

Page 118
Blockfront chest of drawers, mahogany (pine secondary), c. 1770, Massachusetts. Height 30 1/4 inches, width 36 inches, depth 22 inches. Provenance: originally belonged to John Taylor (1743-1825), a merchant of Salem, MA; descended to Sarah Wingate Taylor of California; Ginsburg & Levy.

Page 119
Easy chair, walnut, 1740-60, Rhode Island. Height 48 inches, width 32 inches, depth 24 inches. Provenance: Israel Sack.

Page 120
Chest of drawers, mahogany, c. 1770, America. Height 31 1/4 inches, width 36 inches, depth 21 1/4 inches. I am grateful to Brock Jobe for sharing his observations on this piece with me. Provenance: ex coll. American Wing, Metropolitan Museum of Art; Israel Sack.

Page 121
Chest of drawers, cherry, c. 1790, Connecticut. Height 35 1/4 inches, width 42 1/2 inches, depth 21 1/4 inches. Provenance: Ginsburg & Levy.

Page 122
"Grandmother" clock, signed by Allen Kelley (w. 1810-30), mahogany, c. 1810, Sandwich, MA (case in the manner of Boston and Roxbury). Height 61 1/2 inches, width 14 3/4 inches, depth 8 1/2 inches. Exhibited: Metropolitan Museum, 1930. Provenance: ex coll. Metropolitan Museum; Joe Kindig III.

Page 124
Miniature slant-front desk, walnut and walnut veneer, c. 1760, Pennsylvania. Height 16 inches, width 16 inches, depth 10 1/4 inches. Provenance: Joe Kindig III.

Page 125
Miniature high-post bed, mahogany, c. 1770, Philadelphia. Height 15 1/2 inches, width 10 1/2 inches, depth 14 3/4 inches. Ticking and bolster under new spread are possibly original. Provenance: ex coll. Reginald M. Lewis, Easton, MD; Joe Kindig III.

Page 126
Miniature extension table, curly maple, 1800-10, probably New York or New Jersey. Height 8 inches, width 16 inches, depth 8 inches (closed), 34 3/4 inches (fully extended). Exhibited: Loan Exhibition of

Miniature Furniture, Philadelphia Antiques Show, April 1974. Provenance: Israel Sack.

Page 127

Miniature bed, curly maple, 1800-20, Pennsylvania. Height 14 inches, length 15 1/2 inches. See Hornor, pp. 43-44, for comments about furniture woods in Pennsylvania. Provenance: Willowdale Antiques, Kennett Square, PA.

Page 128

Child's comb-back windsor armchair, 1790-1800, New England. Height 24 3/4 inches, width 17 1/2 inches, depth 10 3/4 inches. Exhibited: Monmouth County Historical Society, Freehold, NJ. Provenance: ex colls. Mrs. J. Amory Haskell of New York City and Red Bank, NJ and Mitchel Taradash, Ardsley-on-Hudson, NY; Diana H. Bittel Antiques, Wynnewood, PA.

Miniature porringer-top tea table, mahogany, 1740-60, Newport. Height 8 1/4 inches, width 13 inches, depth 9 1/2 inches. Illustrated: Schiffer, *Miniature Antique Furniture,* 1972, Pl. 265. Provenance: descended in the Brown-Ives family of Newport, much of whose furniture, according to Sack, was ordered from John Goddard and John Townsend; ex coll. Robert Lee Gill; Israel Sack.

Page 129

Miniature serpentine-front chest of drawers with blocked ends, mahogany, 1780-1800, Massachusetts. Height 13 3/4 inches, width 16 3/4 inches, depth 11 inches. Provenance: Israel Sack.

Miniature chest of drawers, mahogany and birch veneers, 1790-1810, Massachusetts or New Hampshire. Height 9 1/4 inches, width 11 1/2 inches, depth 5 1/2 inches. Provenance: Israel Sack.

Page 130

Miniature two-drawer chest, mahogany, c. 1750, Boston. Height 11 3/4 inches, width 15 1/4 inches, depth 8 1/2 inches. Provenance: Joe Kindig III.

Miniature blanket chest, cherry with light-wood inlays and paint, 1780-1800, Pennsylvania. Height 12 inches, width 17 1/4 inches, depth 10 inches. Provenance: ex coll. Lansdell K. Christie, Long Island, NY, who made a fortune mining iron ore in Africa and became a collector of French furniture and Fabergé objects. When he turned his attention to American antiques, he amassed an important collection whose special focus was Rhode Island furniture; Israel Sack.

Page 131

Miniature tall chest, cherry, 1780-1800, Chester County, PA. Height 22 1/2 inches, width 15 1/2 inches, depth 10 1/4 inches. Provenance: ex coll. Helen Janssen Wetzel; Sotheby's, October 4, 1980; Israel Sack.

Blanket chest, walnut (poplar secondary), 1760-90, Pennsylvania. Height 9 inches, width 18 1/2 inches, depth 8 1/4 inches. Brasses are original. Provenance: Bernard & Dean Levy.

Bibliography

Published Sources

American Antiques from the Israel Sack Collection. 9 vols. Alexandria, VA: Highland House Publishers, 1969-1989.

"Antiques in Domestic Settings: The Home of Mr. and Mrs. Charles K. Davis." *The Magazine Antiques* 39 (January 1941), pp. 18-21; 39 (March 1941), pp. 126-128.

Biddle, James. *American Art from American Collections.* New York, NY: Metropolitan Museum of Art, 1963.

Blair, Raymond N. "The making of Joe Hennage, printer," *Printing Management,* 1971.

British Federation of Master Printers. *Members Circular.* July 1971, p. 166.

Buhler, Kathryn C. *American Silver: 1655-1825 in the Museum of Fine Arts Boston.* 2 vols. Boston: Museum of Fine Arts, Boston, 1972.

Buhler, Kathryn C. and Hood, Graham. *American Silver: Garvan and Other Collections in the Yale University Art Gallery.* 2 vols. New Haven: Yale University Press, 1970.

Burton, E. Milby. *Charleston Furniture 1700-1825.* Charleston, SC: The Charleston Museum, 1955.

Chippendale, Thomas. *The Gentleman and Cabinet-Maker's Director.* London: Thomas Chippendale, 1754.

Colonial Society of Massachusetts. *Boston Furniture of the Eighteenth Century: A Conference Held by the Colonial Society of Massachusetts, 1972.* Charlottesville, VA: University Press of Virginia, 1974.

Comstock, Helen. *American Furniture: Seventeenth, Eighteenth, and Nineteenth Century Styles.* New York: The Viking Press, 1962.

————————. *The Looking Glass in America, 1700-1825.* New York: The Viking Press, 1968.

————————. "More about looking glasses," *The Magazine Antiques* 87 (May 1965), pp. 592-593.

Cooke, Edward S., Jr., ed. *Upholstery in America & Europe from the Seventeenth Century to World War I.* New York: W.W. Norton & Co., 1987.

Cooper, Wendy A. *In Praise of America: American Decorative Arts, 1650-1830/ Fifty Years of Discovery Since the 1929 Girl Scouts Loan Exhibition.* New York: Alfred A. Knopf, 1980.

Deák, Gloria-Gilda. *Picturing America, 1497-1899: Prints, Maps, and Drawings bearing on the New World Discoveries and on the Development of the Territory that is now the United States.* Princeton, NJ: Princeton University Press, 1988.

Eckhardt, George H. *Pennsylvania Clocks and Clockmakers: An Epic of Early American Science, Industry, and Craftsmanship.* New York: The Devin-Adair Company, 1955.

Elder, William Voss III and Stokes, Jayne E. *American Furniture, 1680-1880, from the Collection of the Baltimore Museum of Art.* Baltimore, MD: The Baltimore Museum of Art, 1987.

Federhen, Deborah Anne. "The serpentine-front chests of drawers of Jonathan Gostelowe and Thomas Jones," *The Magazine Antiques* 133 (May 1988), pp. 1174-1183.

Flanigan, J. Michael. *American Furniture from the Kaufman Collection.* Washington, D.C.: National Gallery of Art, 1986.

Flynt, Henry N. and Fales, Martha Gandy. *The Heritage Foundation Collection of Silver.* Deerfield, MA.: The Heritage Foundation, 1968.

French, Hollis. *Jacob Hurd and His Sons, Nathaniel and Benjamin, Silversmiths, 1702-1781.* Addenda. Walpole Society, 1941.

Gaines, Edith. "Powell? Potts? Pitts! - the T. P. epergnes," *The Magazine Antiques* 87 (April 1965), pp. 462-465.

Gershenson, Doris Fisher. "Living with Antiques: The Detroit Home of Mr. and Mrs. Charles H. Gershenson," *The Magazine Antiques* 91 (May 1967), pp. 637-641.

Gloag, John. *Georgian Grace: A Social History of Design from 1660 to 1830.* London: Adam and Charles Black, 1956.

Goyne, Nancy A. "The Bureau Table in America," *Winterthur Portfolio* Vol. III. Winterthur, DE: Winterthur Museum, 1967.

Greenlaw, Barry A. *New England Furniture at Williamsburg.* Charlottesville, VA: The University Press of Virginia, 1974.

Harris, Nathaniel. *Chippendale.* Secaucus, NJ: Chartwell Books, 1989.

Heckscher, Morrison H. *American Furniture in The Metropolitan Museum of Art II, Late Colonial Period: The Queen Anne and Chippendale Styles.*

New York: The Metropolitan Museum of Art and Random House, 1985.

——————— "Form and Frame: New Thoughts on the American Easy Chair," *The Magazine Antiques* 100 (December 1971), pp. 886-893.

Hewitt, Benjamin A.; Kane, Patricia E.; and Ward, Gerald A. *The Work of Many Hands: Card Tables in America, 1790-1820.* New Haven, CT: Yale University Art Gallery, 1982.

Hornor, William MacPherson, Jr. *Blue Book: Philadelphia Furniture.* Privately printed,1935. Reprint (containing an introductory essay by Joe Kindig III). Alexandria, VA: Highland House Publishers, 1988.

Howard, David Sanctuary and Ayers, John. *China for the West: Chinese Porcelain and other Decorative Arts for Export Illustrated from the Mottahedeh Collection.* London: Sotheby Parke Bernet, 1978.

Jobe, Brock and Kaye, Myrna. *New England Furniture: The Colonial Era: Selections from the Society for the Preservation of New England Antiquities.* Boston: Houghton Mifflin Co., 1984.

Kane, Patricia E. *Three Hundred Years of American Seating Furniture: Chairs and Beds from the Mabel Brady Garvan and Other Collections at Yale University.* Boston: New York Graphic Society, 1976.

Karrow, Robert W., Jr. *Mapping the American Revolutionary War.* Chicago: The Newberry Library, 1974.

Kindig, Joseph K., III. *The Philadelphia Chair, 1685-1785.* Harrisburg, PA: The Historical Society of York County, 1978.

Kirk, John T. *American Furniture and the British Tradition to 1830.* New York: Alfred A. Knopf, 1982.

"'The Lindens,' Washington Home of Mr. and Mrs. George Maurice Morris," *The Magazine Antiques* 33 (February 1938), pp. 66-68, 76-79.

The Magazine Antiques. New York: Brant Publications, 1948-1990, *passim.*

Monkhouse, Christopher P. and Michie, Thomas S. *American Furniture in Pendleton House.* Providence, RI: Museum of Art, Rhode Island School of Design, 1986.

Montgomery, Charles F. *American Furniture: The Federal Period, in the Henry Francis du Pont Winterthur Museum.* New York: The Viking Press, 1966.

Montgomery, Florence M. *Textiles in America, 1650-1870.* New York: W. W. Norton & Co., 1984.

Morrison, Russell; Papenfuse, Edward C.; Bramucci, Nancy; and Janson-LaPalme, Robert J.H. *On the Map.* Chestertown, MD: Washington College, 1983.

Moses, Michael. *Master Craftsmen of Newport: the Townsends and Goddards.* Tenafly, NJ: MMI Americana Press, 1984.

Mudge, Jean McClure. *Chinese Export Porcelain in North America.* New York: Clarkson N. Potter, 1986.

Ott, Joseph K. "Some Rhode Island Furniture," *The Magazine Antiques* 107 (May 1975), pp. 940-51.

Palmer, Arlene M. *A Winterthur Guide to Chinese Export Porcelain.* New York: Crown Publishers, 1976.

Peirce, Donald C. and Alswang, Hope. *American Interiors: New England and the South: Period Rooms at The Brooklyn Museum.* New York: Universe Books, 1983.

Philadelphia Museum of Art, *Philadelphia Silver, 1682-1800.* Philadelphia: Philadelphia Museum of Art, 1956.

Phillips, John Goldsmith. *China-Trade Porcelain.* Cambridge, MA: Harvard University Press, 1956.

Pleasants, J. Hall and Sill, Howard. *Maryland Silversmiths, 1715-1830.* Baltimore, MD: Lord Baltimore Press, 1930.

Pressland, David. *The Art of the Tin Toy.* New York: Crown Publishers, Inc., 1976.

Puig, Francis J. and Conforti, Michael. *The American Craftsman and the European Tradition 1620-1820.* Hanover, NH: University Press of New England, 1989.

Quimby, Ian M. G., ed. *American Furniture and Its Makers. Winterthur Portfolio,* Vol. XIII. Chicago and London: University of Chicago Press, 1979.

Ring, Betty. "Checklist of looking-glass and frame makers and merchants known by their labels," *The Magazine Antiques* 119 (May 1981), pp. 1178-1195.

Roque, Oswaldo Rodriguez. *American Furniture at Chipstone.* Madison, WI: The University of Wisconsin Press, 1984.

Sack, Albert. *Fine Points of Furniture: Early American.* New York: Crown Publishers, 1950.

Sack, Harold with Wilk, Max. *American Treasure Hunt: The Legacy of Israel Sack.* Boston: Little, Brown and Co., 1986.

Sanchez-Saavedra, E. M. *A Description of the Country: Virginia's Cartographers and Their Maps 1607-1881.* Richmond: Virginia State Library, 1975.

Schiffer, Herbert F. and Peter B. *Miniature Antique Furniture.* Wynnewood, PA: Livingston Publishing Company, 1972.

Sheraton, Thomas. *The Cabinet Dictionary.* London: W. Smith, 1803.

——————— *The Cabinet-maker and Upholsterer's Drawing-book in Four Parts.* London: T. Hensley, 1802.

Shirey, Orville. "Serving Buyers Who Are Hard to Please," *Printing Magazine,* March 1960, p. 74.

Smith, Robert C. "Architecture and sculpture in nineteenth-century mirror frames," *The Magazine Antiques* 109 (February 1976), pp. 350-59.

Stillinger, Elizabeth. *The Antiquers.* New York: Alfred A. Knopf, 1980.

——————— "Profile of a Collector: Katharine Prentis Murphy," *Maine Antique Digest,* November 1983, pp. 8-B, 19-B.

Swan, Mabel Munson. "American Slab Tables," *The Magazine Antiques* 63 (January 1953), pp. 40-43.

Talbott, Page. "Boston Empire Furniture," *The Magazine Antiques* Part I, 107 (May 1975), pp. 878-887; Part II, 109 (May 1976), pp. 1004-1013.

Tooley, R.V. *The Mapping of America.* London: The Holland Press Limited, 1980.

Verner, Coolie. "The Fry and Jefferson Map," *Imago Mundi,* Vol. XXI (1967). Amsterdam: N. Israel.

Wadsworth Atheneum. *Connecticut Furniture, Seventeenth and Eighteenth Centuries.* Hartford, CT: Wadsworth Atheneum, 1967.

Ward, Gerald W. R. *American Case Furniture in the Mabel Brady Garvan and Other Collections at Yale University.* New Haven, CT: Yale University Art Gallery, 1988.

Warren, David B. *Bayou Bend: American Furniture, Paintings and Silver from the Bayou Bend Collection.* Boston: New York Graphic Society, 1975.

Winchester, Alice. "Living with Antiques: the home of Mr. and Mrs. Mitchel Taradash," *The Magazine Antiques* 63 (January 1953), pp. 44-47.

——————. "Living with Antiques: the New York apartment of Mrs. Andrew Varick Stout," *The Magazine Antiques* 79 (May 1961), pp. 470-473.

——————. "Living with Antiques: the Washington home of Mrs. George Maurice Morris," *The Magazine Antiques* 69 (January 1956), pp. 60-63.

Unpublished Sources

Personal interviews with Betsy and Wendell Garrett, June and Joe Hennage, Trudy Moyles, and Harold Sack about the Hennages. Personal interviews with Mary Humelsine about the Hennages' early involvement with Colonial Williamsburg. Personal interviews with Elizabeth Blagojevitch, John Davis, Mary Humelsine and Alice Winchester about the development of the Antiques Forum.

Hennage, Joseph H. Unpublished lecture, "Building a House for a Collection."

Winchester, Alice. Unpublished lecture, "Women Collectors and the American Decorative Arts."